The Vocation of Man

JOHANN GOTTLIEB FICHTE

The Vocation of Man

Translated, With Introduction and Notes, by
Peter Preuss

HACKETT PUBLISHING COMPANY
Indianapolis/Cambridge

Johann Gottlieb Fichte: 1762–1814
The Vocation of Man was originally published in 1800.

Cover design by Listenberger Design Associates
Interior design by Elizabeth Shaw Editorial and Publishing Services

Library of Congress Cataloging-in-Publication Data
Fichte, Johann Gottlieb, 1762–1814.
The vocation of man.

...nslation of: Die Bestimmung des Menschen.
Bibliography: p.
1. Man. 2. Faith. I. Preuss, Peter, 1939–
II. Title.
B2844.B52E5   1987   128   87-3610
ISBN-13: 978-0-87220-038-8
ISBN-13: 978-0-87220-037-1 (pbk.)

For further information, please address
Hackett Publishing Company, Inc.
P.O. Box 44937
Indianapolis, Indiana 46244-0937

www.hackettpublishing.com

Contents

TRANSLATOR'S INTRODUCTION

It doesn't really matter whether we see the history of modern philosophy as a series of failures in face of skepticism or as progress spurred on by skepticism, for the progress is only in the ingenuity of the failures anyway. When Fichte was a student, the dominant philosophy was that of Kant, which may be seen as an attempt to overcome Humean skepticism. When Fichte wrote about the relationship of these two philosophies in 1792,[1] it is clear that he considered both Hume and Kant skeptics. Hume he took to be a Pyrrhonian skeptic, for he saw him as leaving open the possibility of theoretical understanding of reality. Kant he took to be a "negative dogmatist," i.e., an academic skeptic, for he took him to have shown the impossibility of theorical knowledge of reality. Fichte also understands his own theoretical philosophy, transcendental idealism, to be skepticism in a modern idiom. In the ancient world, skepticism had been the way out of philosophy for philosophers who had been deeply disappointed by philosophy's pretensions to a wisdom it did not possess. In Fichte's day, skepticism was needed as a way out of the dogmatic philosophy which provided the basis of the new physics.

The dogmatic philosophy which is the target of Fichte's skepticism is the deterministic materialism of the eighteenth century and,

---

1. "Recension des Aenesidemus, etc.," written in 1792, published in 1794 in *Jenaer Allgemeine Literaturzeitung*, no. 47–49, cf. di Giovanni, George and Harris, H.S., *Between Kant and Hegel*, State University of New York Press, 1985, p. 147, (the last paragraph).

beyond that, the philosophy of Spinoza. While this materialism seemed to give an intellectually satisfying theoretical understanding of reality, it made nonsense of the human adventure in the world by equating it with any other natural event. No one has ever been more deeply offended by the loss of freedom, i.e., the loss of humanity, entailed by universal determinism than Fichte. *The Vocation of Man* not only includes perhaps the finest statement of determinism in the literature, but also the most eloquent lament in face of its consequences.

Book One presents deterministic materialism. Book Two presents transcendental idealism as a skeptical dismantling of the new dogmatism. Fichte is quite clear that idealism is not meant to be a new philosophy, a new theoretical understanding, a new dogmatism. It is merely an intellectual exercise open to anyone who accepts the autonomy of theoretical reason. Its function is to destroy the current deterministic dogma. But if it were now itself to become a theoretical understanding of reality it would be every bit as bad. While human life is no longer seen as a mere natural event it would now be seen as a mere dream. We would be no more human in the one understanding than the other. In the one understanding I am the material to which life happens as an event, in the other I am the uninvolved spectator of the dream which is my life. Fichte finds each of these to be equal cause for lament. No, the task is not to replace one theoretical philosophy with another one, but to get out of philosophy altogether. Philosophical reason is not autonomous, but has its foundation in practical reason, i.e., the will.

When Fichte wrote *The Vocation of Man* he had just been dismissed from his professorship at Jena on a charge of atheism. He had left his wife and young son in Jena and moved to Berlin at the invitation of Friedrich Schlegel, a leading figure of German romanticism, who had rented rooms for him. It took him three days to travel from Jena to Berlin (July 1–3, 1799) and, while short of money, he was relieved of "a lot of money" along the way on various pretexts. When he finally arrived in Berlin, that "immense, dusty, tiring city," he found his rooms "pleasant enough" but infested with bedbugs. His mood was low.

But it didn't last. Summer and fine weather had come to Berlin. Fichte went for long walks in the city and soon in the surrounding countryside as well. His health improved, he even lost his chronic cough, and soon he felt healthy and fit. He seems, at least initially, to have enjoyed the bohemian circle of young romantics to which he was introduced by Schlegel. He even contemplated moving into larger accommodations with some of them and sharing a cook to reduce expenses. But his wife, who was invited to move in as well, seems to have disapproved, so the idea was dropped.

It seemed that Fichte would have to earn a living by writing, since he neither would nor could return to his job in Jena and efforts to secure a professorship in Heidelberg were unsuccessful. But that didn't upset him. In fact he seemed rather to look forward to it, and his mood was increasingly optimistic. He had begun writing *The Vocation of Man* and was uncommonly pleased with how well it was going. He was now writing as a private philosopher rather than a professor. He was writing in nontechnical language for a wider audience than the professional. He seemed almost relieved to be able to do so, to express himself with a sincerity which the artificiality of the technical language of the professional would not allow. The disdain for the technical prose of the professional, which is evident in *The Vocation of Man,* is not sour grapes. Two years earlier, in a letter to his fellow philosopher Reinhold, dated March 21, 1797, he had already indicated that the technical language of his major work, *The Science of Knowledge,* was its weakest feature. One could, for example, master the language and miss the meaning, and in the academic world this sort of thing happened all too often. In fact he thought that there was no limit to the different ways in which his doctrine could be presented. Each person, he wrote, would have to think it differently, in his own way, in order to understand it properly. For it to be understood required more than a careful reading of the text; it also required an inner contribution by the reader. Only with existentialists like Kierkegaard and Jaspers does such a consideration reappear in the subsequent history of philosophy, and Plato's seventh letter comes to mind as a precursor in antiquity. To present the heart of his philosophy in various ways would make it easier for readers to get beyond the letter to the meaning, Fichte thought, and already in 1797 he projected such a variety of presentations.

His situation in 1799 provided the opportunity to present his philosophy in plain language. The technical thought of professional philosophers, which is expressed in technical philosophical language, has no meaning or content as such, he wrote to Reinhold on April 22, 1799. Its value lies in a further meaning which is thought in it, and which may also be conceived otherwise. In fact, technical philosophical thought, he wrote, is merely the instrument with which to produce the work and which, once the work is done and the meaning grasped, may be discarded as useless. And now, in Berlin, he would see whether what he had to say could not be said more clearly and made more intelligible in plain language. His aim, he wrote to Reinhold on May 22, 1799, was to raise his system to greater intelligibility, to be better and more widely understood. His opponents, he wrote, did not persecute an atheist in him but "a free thinker who is beginning to make himself understood." Kant had already tried to present the same message, thought Fichte, but Kant's good fortune was his obscurity.

Fichte's philosophical message is roughly this: The aim of philosophy is to make reality intelligible, to explain our experience of the world. There are two basic ways in which such an explanation could go and, therefore, two basic types of philosophy. Either we begin with things, a world of matter, which (by natural evolution perhaps) produces conscious beings, which it then affects in various ways to cause experience in them. This option is presented in Book One of *The Vocation of Man*. Or we begin with minds, which produce their own experiences according to the laws of their own constitution. This option is presented in Book Two as the skeptical dismantling of the first option and it is also briefly considered as a philosophical option in its own right. The first type of philosophy is realism or materialism. The second type is idealism. Fichte is widely misunderstood as opting for idealism over realism. It is pointed out, of course, that what Fichte opts for is not just idealism but "transcendental idealism" or even "absolute idealism." But this obscures Fichte's main point—namely, that neither realism (of whatever kind) nor idealism (of whatever kind) yields knowledge, theoretical understanding of reality. Both yield unacceptable nonsense if taken to their final conclusions. And precisely this yields the valuable insight that the intellect is not autonomous. The intellect, to function properly as part of a whole human being, must relate to the activity of that being. Human beings do contemplate and try to understand reality, but not from a standpoint outside the world. Human beings are in the world and it is as agents in the world that we require an understanding of the world. The intellect is not autonomous but has its foundation in our agency, in practical reason or the will.

The will provides this foundation in two ways. First, in an act of faith it transforms the apparent picture show of experience into an objective world of things and of other people. The use of the word "faith" should not suggest a kind of Kierkegaardian collapse into orthodox religion. Rather, faith indicates a free (i.e., theoretically unjustifiable) act of mind by which the conditions within which we can act and use our intellects first come to be for us. In *The Science of Knowledge* Fichte preferred to use the term "creative imagination." And second, it is the conscience which provides us with commands of action.

In none of this is the old philosophical ambition of attaining true knowledge of intelligible reality realized, of course. Our theoretical pursuit ends in total cognitive skepticism and remains there. Instead we are provided with the practical fictions, held by faith or creative imagination, of an objective world as the common sphere of the moral activity of a number of free finite wills, of a supersensible world beyond the objective sensible one in which we exist even now and in which the truly important effects of our moral activity occur, and of an infinite will as the true author of our moral duty and vocation. These fictions allow, within limits, a kind of practical understanding of the objective world which is quite compatible with philosophical skepticism. Carneades, the head of the Platonic Academy two centuries after Plato, had already seen this in the ancient world when he pointed out to dogmatic Stoics the best kind of probabilist knowledge they were capable of.[2] In the modern world this kind of practical understanding was developed enormously as empirical science.

And these fictions also allow a practical consciousness of myself as a task. Among the very few significant innovations of modern philosophy is the conception of human historicity. This is the view

2. cf. Sextus Empiricus, *Against the Logicians* I, 176–189.

that a human being is not a substance with a permanent nature who behaves in accordance with this nature in much the way a machine works according to its design. Rather, a human being is basically the activity, the task of making himself be what he will be within a given situation. This thought is not new with Fichte. It was already anticipated by the 15th-century humanist Pico della Mirandola in his *Oration*. But with Pico it was an isolated thought without further effect. Such things occur in philosophy. Tertullian stumbled across the relation of religious faith to absurdity around 200 A.D., but it had no effect until Kierkegaard developed it. St. Augustin stumbled across the *cogito* around 400 A.D., but its importance did not become apparent until Descartes developed it. Just so Pico had stumbled across the idea of human historicity, but not until Fichte and the subsequent existentialist tradition was the idea developed.

Fichte's philosophy ends in total cognitive skepticism, i.e., in the abandonment of philosophy proper, and looks for wisdom instead to a kind of quasi-religious faith. But he thinks that this is not a problem, since all that matters is practical: to produce a world fit for human beings, and to produce myself as the person I would be for all eternity. The solid support for this is Fichte's view that my conscience clearly and infallibly tells me the right thing to do on every occasion. And this belief in the clarity and infallibility of conscience is accompanied by the background belief in the goodness and competence of an infinite will acting in this world and the next like a benevolent omniscient divine providence. But Fichte is among the very last philosophers to hold such innocent views. In this century these views have become deeply problematical. The situation of contemporary philosophy not only includes something like Fichte's insight into the ultimate theoretical unintelligibility of the world and ourselves, but also the loss of his comforting moral certainty.

When *The Vocation of Man* was published early in 1800, it was not received as well and as widely as Fichte had hoped. Despite the plain language, people still found it difficult. Reinhold wrote to Fichte on March 1, 1800, that he had read the book and along with the normal pleasantries he also indicated that there were parts he did not understand. Others also read the book and found it more difficult than they had anticipated. Schleiermacher, a friend of

Fichte and a theologian, wrote a problematical review of it. For the rest of his career Fichte wrote both in technical professional language and in popular plain language, but he was never satisfied that he had finally made himself understood.

Despite its nontechnical style, the thought presented in *The Vocation of Man* is far from simple. The book must be read carefully, but it will repay close reading.

For his meticulous reading of the manuscript and many valuable suggestions, I am pleased to thank Peter Heath.

The University of Lethbridge   Peter Preuss
Alberta, Canada

SELECTED BIBLIOGRAPHY

Fichte's Principal Works
Versuch einer Kritik aller Offenbarung (1792)
Grundlage der gesammten Wissenschaftslehre (1794)
Grundlage des Naturrechts (1796)
Das System der Sittenlehre (1798)
Über den Grund unseres Glaubens an eine göttliche Weltregierung
   (1798)
Die Bestimmung des Menschen (1800)
Die Grundzüge des gegenwärtigen Zeitalters (1804)
Die Anweisung zum seligen Leben (1806)
Reden an die deutsche Nation (1808)
Die Staatslehre (1813)

Recent Translations
Attempt At a Critique of All Revelation, translated by Garrett Green,
   Cambridge University Press, Cambridge 1978
The Science of Knowledge, edited and translated by Peter Heath and
   John Lachs, Cambridge University Press, Cambridge 1982
Recent scholarly work on Fichte in English is confined to profes-
   sional Journals. *Idealistic Studies* devoted its whole Vol. VI, no. 2,
   May 1976 to Fichte.

NOTE ON THE TEXT

The German text of *Die Bestimmung des Menschen* from which the present translation was made is the 1971 republication from Walter de Gruyter and Co. of the 1845/46 edition of Fichte's works prepared by his son Immanuel Hermann Fichte. The text and the translation were checked against the Bavarian Academy Edition of 1981 and pertinent differences indicated in footnotes. The only other translation into English is by William Smith, done in 1848 and still widely available.

PREFACE

This book is intended to give an account of recent philosophy so far as it is useful outside the schools, and to present that philosophy in the order in which it would develop without artifice in straightforward reflection on the matter. The more technical apparatus of philosophy, intended to meet the objections and extravagances of over-refined thought, will remain beyond the scope of the present work, as will whatever is only the foundation for other positive sciences and, finally, whatever is just a matter of pedagogy in the widest sense, i.e., of the thoughtful and deliberate education of mankind. Those objections are not raised by the natural understanding, which leaves positive science to professionals and the education of mankind, so far as this depends on people, to teachers and government officials.

This book, then, is not intended for professional philosophers who will find nothing in it which has not already been presented in other writings by the same author. It is meant to be intelligible to all readers who are at all capable of understanding a book. Doubtless it will be found to be unintelligible by those who just want to learn a few fine phrases which they can then repeat with some variation, and who think that this memorization is the same thing as understanding.

This essay is meant to attract the reader, to engage his interest and powerfully move him from the sensible world to the supersensible. The author, for his part, did not go to work without enthusiasm. The ardor with which one begins a project often dwindles

1

with the effort required to execute it. In the same way, one runs the risk of being unfair to oneself once the work is done. In short, whether the book succeeds in its intention or not can only be decided by the effect it will have on those readers for whom it was meant, and the author has no voice in this.

I still need to remind a few readers that the "I" who speaks in the book is by no means the author. Rather, the author wishes that the reader may come to see himself in this "I"; that the reader may not simply relate to what is said here as he would to history, but rather that while reading he will actually converse with himself, deliberate back and forth, deduce conclusions, make decisions like his representative in the book, and through his own work and reflection, purely out of his own resources, develop and build within himself the philosophical disposition that is presented to him in this book merely as a picture.

BOOK ONE
Doubt

On the whole, I think that by now I know a good deal of the world around me; and indeed I have made enough of an effort and taken sufficient care in acquiring this knowledge. I have given credence only to the confirmation of my senses, only to consistent experience. I have touched what I have seen, I have taken apart what I have touched; I have repeated my observations again and again; I have compared the various appearances with each other; and I was satisfied only after I had insight into their exact connection, only after I could explain one by the other and deduce one from the other, being able to calculate the results in advance and confirm by observation that the results occurred as I had calculated them. I am, therefore, as sure of the accuracy of this part of my knowledge as I am of my own existence; I walk about firmly in that part of my world with which I am acquainted and at every moment stake my existence and well-being on the validity of my convictions.

But—what am I myself, and what is my vocation?

Superfluous question! It was a long time ago that my instruction on this point came to an end, and it would take time to recall everything I have explicitly heard, learned, and believed about it.

Then in what way did I arrive at this knowledge which I vaguely remember that I have? Did I, driven by a burning desire to know, work my way through uncertainty, through doubt and contradictions? Did I, when I came across something plausible, withhold my assent, test and test again this probability, clarify it, and compare it—until an inner voice unmistakably and irresistibly called to me:

"It is so and not otherwise, as surely as you live and breathe?" No, I remember nothing like that. That instruction was given to me before I felt any want for it; I was given an answer before I had raised a question. I listened because I could not avoid it; how much got stuck in my memory was a matter of chance; without examination and without taking any interest I just let things come as they might.

So how could I persuade myself that indeed I have some knowledge about this object of reflective thought? If I only know what I am convinced of and have found out myself, if I really know only what I have experienced myself, then indeed I cannot say that I have the least knowledge about my vocation; I only know what others claim to know about it; and all I can say here with any assurance is that I have heard people say such and such about these matters.

So far then, while I investigated trivial things myself with exacting care, I have depended on the trustworthiness and care of strangers in matters of the highest importance. I credited others with an interest, a seriousness and exactness in the highest concerns of mankind which I have by no means found in myself. I have had an indescribably higher regard for them than for myself.

How else could they have got whatever true knowledge they have except by their own thoughtful reflection? And why should not I, by the same thoughtful reflection, find the same truth, since I am as much as they are? How much have I underestimated and despised myself till now!

I don't want this to be so any longer! At this moment I will claim my rights and assume my proper dignity. Let everything alien be given up. I will investigate *for myself.* It could be that I will find in myself secret wishes about how the investigation may end, an inclination to give preference to certain assertions; if so, I shall forget and deny this inclination and grant it no influence on the direction of my thoughts. I want to go to work *with rigor and care* and accept any result honestly. What I find to be true, whatever it may be, I shall welcome. I want to *know.* With the same assurance with which I count on the floor to support me when I step on it, and on the fire to burn me were I to approach it, I want to be able to count on what I myself am and what I will be. And should this by any chance not be possible, then I want at least to know that it is not possible.

And I will submit even to this result of the investigation, should it disclose itself to me as the truth. I hurry to solve my problem.

I take hold of nature as it hurries past in its flight. I stop it for a moment, pay close attention to the present moment, and reflect on it. I think about this nature with respect to which my powers of thought have hitherto been developed and about which I have formed conclusions valid in its domain.

I am surrounded by objects which I am constrained to regard as self-subsisting things, separated from each other: I see plants, trees, animals. To each particular thing I ascribe properties and peculiarities by which I distinguish them from each other. To this plant I ascribe such a form, to another plant a different one; to this tree I ascribe leaves shaped in a particular way, to another leaves of a different shape.

Each object has *its definite number* of properties, no more, no less. If you know an object completely then you will be able to answer every question about whether the object is this or that with a decisive yes or no which puts an end to all vacillation between being and nonbeing. Everything there is, either *is or is not something:* it is colored or not colored, has a particular color or doesn't have it, is tasty or not tasty, is tangible or not tangible, and so on indefinitely.

Each object possesses each of these properties *to a definite degree.* If there is a measure for a particular property, and if I am able to apply it, then I will find a certain quantity of this property which it does not exceed in the slightest nor fall short of. Suppose I measure the height of a tree; there is a definite height, and the tree is neither higher nor lower by a single line than it is. Consider the green of its leaves; it is a definite green, not in the slightest darker or brighter, more vivid or more faded than it is, even if I have neither the measure nor the word for it. Consider this plant: it is at a definite stage between sprouting and maturity, neither closer nor further from either one than it is. *All that there is, is determinate through and through; it simply is what it is and nothing else.*

I don't wish to claim, of course, that I cannot think of something hovering halfway between two incompatible properties. I do after all think of indeterminate objects, and more than half of my thinking consists of such thoughts. I think of a tree in general. Does this tree have fruit or not, leaves or not; and, should it have some, what is their number? To what species of tree does it belong? How tall is it? And so on. All these questions remain unanswered and my thinking is in those respects indeterminate as surely as I did not intend to think of a particular tree but of a tree in general. Only, I deny that this tree in general really exists just because it is indeterminate. Everything real has its definite number of all possible properties of real things, and has each of them to a certain degree as surely as it is real; although I will admit that perhaps there is not a single object whose properties I can exhaustively identify and measure.

But nature hurries on in its constant change. And while I am still talking about the moment I seized upon, it has already gone and everything has changed; and before I seized it, everything was likewise different. Things had not always been as they were and as I had seized upon them, but they had become so.

Why, then, and from what cause did things come to be just the way they did; why did nature, from the infinitely various determinations which are possible for it, assume at this moment exactly the one it actually assumed, and not others?

For this reason: because they were preceded by exactly those conditions which in fact preceded them and no others among the possible ones; and because the present ones followed just these conditions and no other possible ones. Had anything at all been even slightly other than it was in the preceding moment, then in the present moment something would also be other than it is. And what caused everything in the preceding moment to be as it was? This: that in the moment which preceded that one everything was as it was then. And that one moment again depended on the one which preceded *it*; and this last one again on *its* predecessor; and so on indefinitely. Just so, in the next following moment nature will be determined as it will be because in the present moment it is determined as it is; and something would necessarily be different in this next following moment from what it will be, if in the present one even the least thing were other than it is. And in the moment following the next one everything will be as it will be, because in the next one everything will be as it will be; and so its successor will depend on *this next one* just as *it* will depend on its predecessor; and so on indefinitely.

Nature strides through the endless series of its possible determinations without rest; and the alteration of these determinations is not lawless, but strictly lawful. What exists in nature is necessarily as it is, and it is simply impossible that it be any different. I enter into an unbroken chain of appearances, since each link is determined by the one preceding it and determines the one following it; I enter into a tight interconnection since from any given moment I could find all possible conditions of the universe by merely thinking about it. Backward, were I to *explain* that given moment; forward, were I to *infer* others from it; if backward, I would look for the causes through which alone it could become actual, and if forward, I would look for the consequences which it necessarily must have. In every part I receive the whole because every part is only what it is through the whole, and through that it is necessarily what it is.

What is it then that I have just found? In a general overview of my assertions I find their substance to be this: to presuppose, for every case of becoming, a being out of which and through which it came to be; to prefix to each condition another condition, and to every being another being; and never to allow anything to arise from nothing.

Let me dwell on this for a while, develop it, and make quite clear to myself what its content and implications are! For it could easily be that the entire success of my further investigations depends on my clear insight into this point in my reflections.

I began by asking why and from what cause the determinations of objects at this moment are just what they are. I assumed without further proof, and without the least investigation, as something generally known, as something immediately and simply true and certain—as of course it is, and I still think it is and always will—I assumed, I say, that they have a cause; that they have existence and reality not through themselves but through something lying outside of them. I found their existence not sufficient to account for their own existence and found it necessary for their own sake to assume another existence outside of them. Why, I wonder, did I find the existence of those properties or determinations insufficient; why did I find it to be an incomplete existence? What could it be in them that betrays a deficiency to me? Doubtless it is this: in the first place those properties are nothing in and for themselves but are only *in* something else as its qualities; qualities of something qualified, forms of something formed; and something which accepts and supports such qualities—a *substratum* for them, to use the expression of the schools—is always presupposed to make these qualities thinkable. Further, that such a substratum has a definite quality indicates a condition of rest, a halting of its transformations, a cessation of its becoming. If I transpose it into a state of change, then there is no more determinateness in it, but rather a transition from one condition into another opposite one, proceeding through indefiniteness. The state of determinacy of a thing is therefore a state and indication of a mere passivity and a mere passivity is an incomplete existence. An activity is required which corresponds to this passivity, which would explain it, and through and by means of which this passivity first becomes thinkable; or, as one usually expresses this, *which contains the ground of this passivity.*

By no means, therefore, did I think, nor was I constrained to think that the different successive determinations of nature as such bring each other about; that the present state of things would destroy itself and would in the following moment, when it no longer exists, bring forth in its place another state of things which neither is nor is contained in the previous state; a procedure which is quite unthinkable. A state of things neither produces itself nor something else out of itself.

I thought and had to think about an *active force* which is peculiar to the object and constitutes its proper essence, in order to grasp the gradual generation and change of those determinations.

And how do I conceive this force, what is its nature and mode of expression? None other than this, that under these particular circumstances, through itself and for its own sake, it simply produces this particular effect and no other, and produces it surely and without fail.

The principle of activity, of generation and becoming *in and for itself,* is purely in that force itself and not in anything outside it, as surely as it is force; the force is not driven or set in motion, it sets itself in motion. The reason why *it develops in just this particular way* partly lies in it itself because it is this force and no other, and partly outside of it in the circumstances in which it develops. Both of these, the inner determination of the force through itself and the outer determination by circumstances, must unite in order to produce a change. Concerning the first: the circumstances, the static being and enduring of things, produce no becoming for they contain the opposite of all becoming, namely static enduring. Concerning the second: that force, as surely as it is to be thinkable, is thoroughly determinate; but its determinateness is completed by the circumstances in which it develops. I only think a force; a force exists for me only so far as I perceive an effect; an ineffective force, which nevertheless is supposed to be a force and not a static thing, is completely unthinkable. Every effect, however, is determinate, since the effect is only the imprint, only another perspective, on the effective activity itself. The effective force is determined in its activity, and the ground of this determinateness lies partly in itself, because without that it would not be thought of at all as something particular which exists in its own right; and partly outside it, because its own determinateness can only be thought as conditioned.

Here a flower has grown out of the ground and I infer from that a formative force in nature. Such a formative force exists for me only insofar as I am aware of this flower and others, and plants in general and animals; I can describe this force only through its effect, and for me it simply isn't anything other than just that—something which brings about such an effect, that which produces flowers and plants and animals and organic shapes in general. I will further claim that in this spot a flower, this particular flower, could grow only insofar as all the circumstances combined in order to make it possible. This combination of all the circumstances required for its possibility, however, does not at all explain the actuality of the flower yet; in addition I must assume a particular, self-active, original force of nature: and indeed I must surely assume a force which produces flowers; for another force of nature might perhaps have produced something quite different in the same circumstances. I have then reached the following view of the universe.

When I consider the totality of things as a unity, as one nature, then there is one force; when I consider them as separate things then there are several forces which develop according to their inner laws and go through all possible configurations of which they are capable; and all objects in nature are nothing other than those forces themselves determined in a certain way. The expression of each particular natural force is determined—i.e., comes to be what it is—partly by its own essential character, partly by its own past expressions, partly by the expressions of all remaining natural forces to which it is connected; but, since nature is an interconnected whole, it is connected to all of them. By all of this it is irresistibly determined. Once it has happened to become what it is in its essential character and finds expression under these circumstances, its expression necessarily occurs as it does, and it is simply impossible that it be in the slightest different from what it is.

At every moment of its duration nature is an interconnected whole; at every moment *every particular part* of it has to be as it is because *all the rest* are what they are; and you could shift no grain of sand from its spot without thereby, perhaps invisibly to your eyes, changing something in all parts of the immeasurable whole. But *each moment of this duration* is determined by *all past moments* and will determine all *future moments;* and in the present one you can think the position of no grain of sand other than it is without having to think the whole, indefinitely long past and the whole, indefinitely long future to be different. Try it if you like with this grain of wind-driven sand which you can see here. Think of it as lying a few paces further inland. Then the storm which blew it in from the sea would have to have been stronger than it actually was. But then the preceding weather conditions which caused the storm and its strength would have to have been different from what they were, as well as the weather conditions which preceded and determined them; and, if you continue this indefinitely and without limit, you will come upon a quite different temperature of the air than the actual one and a quite different disposition of the bodies which influence this temperature and are influenced by it. Without doubt temperature has a most decisive influence on the fertility and infertility of countries, and through that even directly on the continuation of human life. How can you know—for since it is not granted us to penetrate the inner recesses of nature it is enough to point out possibilities here—how can you know whether in the weather conditions of the universe which would have been required to drive this grain of sand further inland, some one or other of your ancestors would not have died of hunger or frost or heat before he had produced the son from whom you are descended?—that you would therefore not exist and all you plan to do now and in the future would not be, because a grain of sand lies in another spot?

I myself, along with everything I call mine, am a link in this chain of strict necessity. There was a time—so others tell me who lived at the time, and I am constrained by inference to suppose such a time of which I am not directly aware—there was a time when I did not yet exist, and a moment at which I came to be. I existed only for others, not yet for myself. Since then my self-awareness has gradually developed and I have found in myself certain abilities and dispositions, needs, and natural desires. I am a determinate being which came to be at sometime or other.

I did not come to be through myself. It would be the height of folly to suppose that I existed before I existed in order to bring myself into existence. I came to be actual through a force outside myself. And what force should it be other than the general force of nature, since I am a part of nature? The time of my coming to be and the characteristics with which I came to be were determined by this general force of nature; and all the various ways in which these, my inherited characteristics, have found expression since then and will find expression so long as I will exist are determined by the same force of nature. It was impossible for someone else to have come to be instead of me; it was impossible for this one who now has come into existence to be other than he is and will be at any moment of his existence.

That my states happen to be accompanied by consciousness, and that some of them—thoughts, decisions, and the like—even seem to be nothing other than determinations of consciousness alone, must not confuse me in my thinking. It is so by nature that the plant will develop with regularity, that the animal will move purposefully, and that human beings will think. Why should I take exception to recognizing also the last as the expression of an original force of nature, as I do the first and the second? Nothing but astonishment could prevent my doing so, insofar as thinking is after all a far higher and more artful effect of nature than the formation of plants or the peculiar movement of animals. But how could I let my astonishment affect a calm investigation? Of course, I cannot explain how the force of nature produces thought. But, then, can I explain any better how it produces the formation of a plant, the movement of an animal? I am, of course, not going to lapse into the perverse enterprise of deriving thought from a mere arrangement of matter. For could I even explain the formation of the simplest moss in that way? Those original forces of nature are not to be explained at all, nor can they be explained, for everything explainable is to be explained by them. There just happens to be thought, it simply is, just as the formative force of nature just happens to be and simply is. It is in nature; for that which thinks comes to be and develops according to natural laws: it therefore exists by nature. There is an original force of thought in nature just as there is an original formative force.

The original thinking force of the universe progresses and develops itself in all possible determinations of which it is capable, just as the other original natural forces progress and assume all possible configurations. I am a particular determination of the formative force, like the plant; a particular determination of the peculiar motive force, like the animal; and in addition to this a determination of the thinking force: and the union of these three basic forces into one force, into one harmonious development, is the distinguishing characteristic of my species, just as it is the distinguishing feature of the plant world to be merely a determination of the formative force.

Form, peculiar movement, and thought in me do not depend on each other and cannot be derived from each other: I do not think of my form and movement, and of the forms and movements surrounding me, as I do because they are as they are; and conversely they don't become what they are because I think them so, but they are altogether and immediately the harmonious development of one and the same force whose expression necessarily becomes a being of my species in full accord with itself, a force which could be called an anthropogenetic force. A thought simply arises in me, and just as simply the form which corresponds to it, and just as simply the movement corresponding to both. I am not what I am because I think it or will it; nor do I think it or will it because I am it, but I simply am and think both. There is, however, a higher cause of their agreement.

As surely as those original forces of nature are something for themselves and have their own inner laws and purposes, as surely must those of their expressions which have become actual endure for a while and undergo a certain range of transformations, as long as the force is left to itself and is not suppressed by an alien one superior to it. Whatever disappears in the very instant in which it came to be is surely not an expression of a basic force, but only a consequence of the combined operation of several forces. Plants, a particular determination of the formative force of nature, will, when left to themselves, proceed from their first germination to the ripening of seeds. Human beings, a particular determination of all natural forces in unison, will, when left to themselves, proceed from birth to death of old age. This accounts for the duration of the life of plants, as of human beings, as well as the various determinations of these their lives.

This form, this peculiar movement, this thinking, in harmony with each other, this persistence of all those essential properties amid a variety of accidental changes, are mine so far as I am a being of my species.

But, before I came to be, the anthropogenetic force had already presented itself under various external conditions and circumstances. It is these external circumstances which determine the particular manner of its present activity and which therefore contain the cause why just such an individual of my species becomes actual. The same circumstances can never return, for then the whole of nature would have to return and two natures instead of one would come to be: that is why the individuals which once have existed can never exist again. Further, the anthropogenetic force of nature presents itself at the time when I exist as well, under all the circumstances possible at this time. No combination of such circumstances is completely like the one which brought me into being, if the totality of things is not to separate into two exactly similar but unconnected worlds. It is not possible for two exactly similar individuals to exist at the same time. Thereby, then, it is determined what *I, this particular person,* had to be; and the law by which I became who I am has in general been found. I am what the anthropogenetic force *could* become, given that it was what it was, and that it still is what it is outside of me, and that it stands in this particular relation to other contrary forces of nature; and, since this force could become me it necessarily *had* to become me, for it does not contain within itself any conditions which could limit it. I am who I am because in this state of nature as a whole only I and no one else happened to be possible. A mind which had a complete insight into nature would, from its knowledge of a single human being, definitely be able to say what people have ever existed or will ever exist; in one person it would know *all* actual persons. It is this, my connection with the whole of nature, which determines all I was, all I am, and all I will be: and that same mind could infallibly infer from any possible moment of my existence what I was before it and what I will be after it. Whatever I am and become I am and become necessarily, and it is impossible for me to be anything else.

I am indeed most intimately aware of myself as an independent being and as free on many occasions in my life; but this awareness can be explained quite well with the basic principles given in the foregoing, and is fully compatible with the conclusions just established. My immediate consciousness, perception proper, does not extend *beyond myself* and my determinations. Immediately I know only of myself. What I am able to know beyond that I only know through *inference,* in the manner in which I have just inferred the original forces of nature which in no way come within the sphere of my perceptions. *I,* however, that which I call my "I," my person, am not the anthropogenetic force itself but only one of its expressions: and when I am aware *of myself* I am aware only of this expression and not of that force which I only infer because of the need to explain myself. This expression, however, seen as it really is, emanates from an original and independent force and has to be found as such in consciousness. That is why I take myself to be an *independent* being. For just this reason I appear to myself to be *free* on particular occasions in my life, when these occasions are expressions of the independent force which has fallen to my share in my individuality. I appear to myself as *restrained and limited* when, because of a concatenation of external circumstances which occur in time but don't lie in the original limitation of my individuality, I am unable to do something well within my capacity if only my individual force were considered. And I feel *forced* when this individual force is overwhelmed by others opposed to it so that it is constrained to express itself even contrary to its own nature.

Give a tree consciousness and let it grow unchecked; let it spread its branches and bring forth leaves, buds, blossoms, and fruits peculiar to its species. It will surely not feel limited by the circumstance that it just happens to be a tree, a tree of just this species and just this particular tree of this species. It will feel free because in all those expressions it does nothing but what is demanded by its nature; it will not want to do anything else because it can only want what its nature demands. But let its growth be retarded by unfavorable weather, by inadequate nourishment, or by other causes: it will feel limited and restrained because a drive which really lies in its nature is not being satisfied. Tie its freely striving branches to a trellis, impose alien branches on it by grafting: it will feel forced to act a certain way. Its branches will, of course, continue to grow, but not in the direction they would have taken had they been left to themselves; and it will, after all, bear fruit, but not the fruit demanded by its original nature. In *immediate self-consciousness* I appear to myself to be free; in *reflection* on the whole of nature I find that freedom is unfortunately impossible: the former must be subordinated to the latter for it can even be explained by it.

What lofty satisfaction my mind finds in this doctrine! What order, what solid coherence, what an easy overview does it introduce into the whole of my knowledge! Consciousness is here no longer that stranger in nature whose connection with existing things is so incomprehensible; it is at home in nature and even one of its necessary determinations. Nature rises gradually in the determinate order of its productions. In raw matter it is simple being; in organized matter it returns into itself to work upon itself there inside itself, to form itself in the plant, and to move itself in the animal. In man, its greatest masterpiece, it returns into itself to look at itself and observe itself: it duplicates itself in man as it were, and its mere being becomes being and consciousness in union.

How it is that I would have to know of *my own being* and its determinations is easily explained in this connection. My being and my knowledge have the same common ground: my nature in general. There is no being in me which, simply because it is *my* being, does not at the same time know of itself. The consciousness *of physical objects outside of me* becomes equally comprehensible. The forces whose expression constitutes my personality, the formative self-moving and thinking force in me, are not these forces in nature in general but only a particular part of them; and the reason why they are only this part is that outside of me there still is so and so much other being. From the former, the limitation, you can *calculate* the latter, the limiting. Because I am not this or that, which nevertheless belongs into the concatenation of the totality of being, it has to be outside of me; that is how thinking nature reasons and calculates in me. I am immediately conscious of my limitation because it is mine and I only exist because of it; the consciousness of that which limits me, of that which I myself am not, is mediated by the former and flows from it.

Away, then, with those supposed influences and effects of external things upon me through which they are supposed to infuse a knowledge of themselves into me which is not in them and cannot flow out of them. The cause of my assuming something outside of myself does not lie outside of me but inside me, in the limitation of my own person. By means of this limitation the thinking nature in me goes out of itself and gets an overview of the whole of itself, but in every individual from a particular point of view.

In the same way the concept of *thinking beings similar to me* arises in me. I, or the thinking nature in me, thinks thoughts which are supposed to develop out of it as an individual determination of nature, and other thoughts which are not supposed to have developed out of it itself. And so it is in fact. The former, to be sure, are my peculiar individual contribution to the sum of general thinking in nature; the latter are merely inferred from the former as thoughts which, to be sure, must also occur in their sum but, since they are only inferred, not in me but in another thinking being: from here I first *reason* to thinking beings outside me. In short, in me nature becomes aware of itself as a whole; but only by beginning with the individual consciousness of me and continuing from this to a consciousness of general being through explanation according to the principle of sufficient reason—that is, that nature will think the conditions under which alone the shape, the movement, and the thought which constitute my person became possible. The principle of sufficient reason is the point of transition from the particular, which is itself, to the general, which is outside it. The distinguishing characteristic of the two kinds of knowledge is this: the first is immediate perception, the second inference.

In each individual, nature sees itself from a particular point of view. I call myself *I,* and you *you:* you call *yourself* I, and *me* you; for you I lie outside of you, as you lie outside of me for me. Of those things which lie outside me I first understand what limits me directly, and you what limits you directly. From this point we continue on through the next links, but we describe very different series, which may well intersect each other here and there, but nowhere continue next to each other in the same direction. All possible individuals and, therefore, all possible points of view of consciousness become actual. This consciousness of all individuals taken together constitutes the universe's complete consciousness of itself, and there is no other, for only in the individual is there complete determinateness and reality.

The testimony of each individual's consciousness is infallible as long as it really is the consciousness described so far, for this consciousness develops out of the whole lawful course of nature; but nature cannot contradict itself. If there is some mental presentation somewhere, then there also has to be a being corresponding to it, for presentations are only produced along with the production of the being corresponding to them. Each individual's particular consciousness is thoroughly determined, for it is produced by his nature: no one can have different knowledge and a different degree of vividness of that knowledge than he really has. The *content* of his knowledge is determined by the standpoint which he occupies in the universe; its *clarity and vividness* are determined by the greater or lesser degree of activity which the force of humanity is capable of expressing in his person. Give nature a single determination of a person, however trivial it may seem to be, such as the path of a single muscle or the curve of a hair, and if nature had a universal consciousness and could answer you, it would tell you every thought which this person will think throughout his whole conscious time.

The familiar phenomenon which we call *will* becomes equally intelligible with this doctrine. To will is to be immediately conscious of the activity of one of our inner natural forces. The immediate consciousness of a striving of these forces which is not yet activity because it is checked by the striving of contrary forces is the consciousness of inclination or desire; the battle of opposed forces is indecision; the victory of one of them is experienced as making up your mind with a decision. If the striving force is only the one which we have in common with the plant or the animal then a separation and degradation have already resulted in our inner being because our desire is not commensurate with our rank in the order of things but beneath it, and in a certain manner of speaking it may well be called a base desire. If this striving is the whole undivided force of humanity, then the desire is commensurate with our nature and may be called a higher one. The striving of the latter considered in general may appropriately be called a *moral* law. An activity of the latter is a virtuous will and the act following upon it is virtue. A victory of the former without harmony with the latter is impropriety; a victory of the former over the latter, if the latter puts up a struggle, is vice.

The force that wins in each case wins necessarily; its superior weight is determined by the interconnected arrangement of the universe; accordingly the virtue, impropriety, and vice of each individual is irrevocably determined by that same arrangement. Once again give nature the path of a muscle, the curve of a hair in a particular individual, and, if it could think as a whole and answer you, it would be enough to enable nature to list all his good and bad acts from the beginning to the end of his life. But virtue does not for this reason cease to be virtue, and vice vice. The virtuous person is noble, the vicious person is base and despicable. Nevertheless, both follow necessarily from the arrangement of the universe.

There is such a thing as *remorse,* and it is the consciousness of the continuing striving of humanity in me after its defeat, together with the unpleasant feeling that it was defeated, a disturbing but nevertheless precious pledge of our nobler nature. *Conscience,* and its greater or lesser intensity and sensitivity down to its absolute absence in different individuals, also has its origin in this consciousness of our fundamental drive. The baser sort of person is incapable of remorse because humanity does not even have sufficient force in him to put up a struggle against the lower drives. Reward and punishment are the natural consequences of virtue and vice, for the production of new virtue and the prevention of new vice. Through frequent and significant victories, that is, our peculiar force is expanded and strengthened; through lack of all effectiveness or through frequent defeats it becomes ever weaker. Only the concepts 'guilt' and 'responsibility' have no meaning except in

positive law. That person has become guilty and is held responsible
for his transgression who forces society to use artificial external
means to block those of his drives which threaten the general
security.

My investigation is complete and my desire to know is satisfied. I
know what I am and what constitutes the essence of my species. I
am an expression, determined by the universe, of a self-determined
natural force. To gain insight into my particular personal determinations *by means of its causes* is impossible for I cannot penetrate
to the inside of nature. But I become aware of them *immediately*. I
know very well what I am at the present moment; I can for the
most part remember what I have been in the past; and I will, of
course, experience what I will be when I will be it.

It could never occur to me to make use of this discovery in my
activities because I don't act at all but nature acts in me. I cannot
will the intention of making myself something other than what I
am determined to be by nature, for I don't make myself at all but
nature makes me and whatever I become. I can regret, be glad, and
make good resolutions—leaving aside that strictly speaking I cannot do even that either, but rather everything comes to me of itself
when it is determined to come to me—but all my regret and all my
resolutions won't change in the slightest what I must become. Strict
necessity has me in its inexorable power; if it determines me to be a
fool and to be given to vice, then without doubt I will become a fool
and be given to vice; if it determines me to be wise and good, then
without doubt I will be wise and good. It is neither that necessity's
fault or merit nor mine. It is subject to its own laws and I to its.
After realizing this it will be most conducive to my peace of mind to
give up my wishes to it as well, seeing that my being is wholly given
up to it.

Oh these recalcitrant wishes! For why should I any longer deny
the anguish, the revulsion, the horror which gripped my innermost
being as soon as I saw how the investigation would end? I had
solemnly promised myself that my inclination was to have no influence on the direction of my reflections; and indeed I did not consciously allow it any influence. But may I therefore not admit to
myself in the end that this conclusion contradicts my deepest inner-

most intimations, wishes, and demands? And how can I believe in an explanation of my existence which conflicts so decisively with the innermost root of my existence, with the purpose for the sake of which alone I care to live and without which I deplore my existence, despite the correctness and strict precision of the proofs which this reflection seems to me to have?

Why must my heart grieve and be torn apart by something that so completely sets my mind at rest? Since nothing in nature contradicts itself, is only man a contradictory being? Or perhaps not man, but only I and those like me? Should I perhaps have continued in the amiable illusion which enveloped me, maintained myself within the confines of the immediate consciousness of my being, and never have raised the question about its causes, the answer to which now makes me so miserable? But if this answer is right, then I *had* to raise that question; I did not raise it but thinking nature in me raised it. I was determined to misery, and in vain do I bemoan the lost innocence of my spirit which can never return.

But courage! Let all else abandon me, so long as I don't lose my courage. Of course, I cannot give up something which follows from incontrovertible reasons *for the sake of mere inclination,* no matter how deeply rooted in my inner being the inclination may be or how holy it may appear. But perhaps I made a mistake *in the investigation;* perhaps I grasped the sources from which it had to be conducted only partially and have not seen their every side. I ought to repeat the investigation from the opposite end, which would at least give me a place to start. Well, what is it then that repels me so powerfully and pains me so in the result I have found? What is it I wanted to find in its place? Let me then, above all, get quite clear about that inclination to which I appeal.

That I should be determined to be wise and good or a fool and given to vice, and that I can change nothing in this determination, receive no merit from the former, and bear no fault for the latter— that is what filled me with revulsion and horror. That cause of my being and the determination of my being *outside myself,* the expression of which was further determined by causes *outside it*—that was what repelled me so vehemently. That freedom, which was not *my*

own freedom at all but rather that of *an alien force* outside me, and
which even there was only *conditioned* and not wholly freedom—
that freedom was not enough for me. *I myself,* that of which I am
conscious as my self, as my person, and which in that doctrine
appears as a mere expression of something higher—I want to be
independent—not to be in and through another but to be something for myself; and as such I want myself to be the fundamental
cause of all my determinations. The rank which in that doctrine is
given to each original force of nature I want to have for myself,
with the one difference that the manner of my expression not be
determined by alien forces. I want to have an inner peculiar power
to express myself in an infinitely varied manner, just like those
forces of nature, a power that expresses itself just as it expresses
itself for no other reason than simply that it expresses itself in that
way; but not, as with those forces of nature, that it just happens to
occur under those external circumstances.

What then, according to this my wish, shall be the proper seat
and center of that peculiar power of mine? Obviously not my body,
which I will readily allow to be an expression of natural forces, at
least so far as its being is concerned, even if not so far as its further
determinations are concerned; nor my sensuous inclinations, which
I take to be a relation of these forces to my consciousness. So it
must be my thinking and willing. I want to will with freedom according to a freely conceived purpose, and this will, as simply the
most fundamental cause determined by no higher possible cause, is
to move and shape in the first place my body and by means of it the
world which surrounds me. My active natural power is to be in the
service of my will and simply unable to be made to go into action by
anything other than my will. This is how it should be: there is to be
something that is the best when judged by spiritual standards; I am
to have the ability to seek this with freedom until I find it and to
recognize it as such when I have found it; and it is to be my fault if
I have failed to find it. I am to be able to will the best simply
because I will it; and if instead of it I will something else it is to be
my fault. My acts are to result from this will, and without it no acts
of mine are to take place at all, in that there is to be no other
possible power of my acts than my will. Only as determined by my
will and in its service is my power to take a hand in nature. I want
to be the master of nature and it is to be my servant; I want to have

an influence on nature proportional to my power, but nature is to have none on me.

This is the content of my wishes and demands. An investigation that satisfies my understanding has utterly repudiated them. If, according to the former (my wishes and demands) I am to be independent of nature and in general from any law whatever which I do not give to myself, then, according to the latter (the investigation) I am a thoroughly determined link in the chain of nature. The question now is whether a freedom such as I wish is even thinkable and, if it is, whether a thorough-going and complete reflection on the issue may not find reasons that require me to accept this freedom as real and to ascribe it to myself—which would refute the result of the previous investigation.

That I want to be free, in the way indicated, means: I myself want to make myself be whatever I will be. I would, therefore—and this is what is most puzzling and apparently totally incoherent in this conception—I would already have to be, in a certain sense, what I am to become, so that I could make myself be it; I would have to have a double kind of being, of which the first would contain the basis of a determination of the second. If in this connection I observe my immediate self-consciousness in exercising my will, I find the following: I know various possible ways of acting, among which, it seems to me, I can choose whichever I want. I consider them all, think of new ones, clarify each, compare them with each other, and weigh the possibilities. Finally I choose one from among all of them, determine my will accordingly, and from this resolution of the will there follows the corresponding act. Here, to be sure, it is merely in thinking of my purpose that I *already am* what I will thereafter and as a consequence of this thinking *really* be through willing and acting; I am first as a thinker what in virtue of this thinking I subsequently am as an agent. I make myself: my being through my thinking; my thinking simply through thinking.

You can also postulate a condition of indeterminateness before the determinate condition of an expression of a mere natural force such as a plant, an indeterminate condition in which is given a wealth of various determinations which it might assume if left to itself. The basis of this manifold possibility, to be sure, is *in it*, in its peculiar force, but not *for it*, because it is incapable of concepts. It cannot choose, it cannot through itself put an end to indeterminateness; external determining causes are required to limit it to one among all possible ones, one to which it cannot limit itself. In a plant its determination cannot occur before its determination because it has only one way of being determined—according to its real being. That is why above I was constrained to claim that the expression of every force had to receive its complete determination from outside. Doubtless I thought only of those forces which only express themselves through a being but are incapable of consciousness. The above claim is valid for them without the slightest restriction. In the case of intelligences, however, the reason for this claim does not occur and it seems rash, therefore, to extend it to them as well.

Freedom, in the sense demanded above, is thinkable only in intelligences, but in them it is thinkable without doubt. With this presupposition, man as well as nature is still completely comprehensible. My body and my capacity for acting in the world of the senses are, just as in the above system, expressions of limited natural forces; and my natural inclinations are the relations of these expressions to my consciousness. The mere knowledge of what there is without any contribution from me is generated here, with the presupposition of freedom, just as it was in that system; and up to this point they both agree. According to that earlier system, however—and here the disagreement of the two doctrines begins— my capacity for activity in the sensible world remains in the servitude of nature, is constantly put in motion by the same force which also produced it, and thought is everywhere only a spectator. In the present system this capacity, once it exists, is in the servitude of a power which is higher than nature and quite free of its laws, the power of purposes, and the will. Thought is no longer a mere spectator, but the act itself flows from it. There, in the first system, it is external forces invisible to me that put an end to my indecision and reduce my activity and the immediate consciousness of that activity, i.e., my will, to perfect congruence, just as they are in a plant whose activity is not determined by itself. Here, in the present system, it is I myself, independent and free of the influence of all external forces, who put an end to my indecision determined by the knowledge of what is best, a knowledge produced freely within myself.

Which of the two opinions shall I adopt? Am I free and independent, or am I nothing in myself and merely the appearance of an alien force? It has just become clear to me that neither of the two claims is sufficiently justified. Nothing but its mere thinkability speaks in favor of the first one; and for the second one I take a proposition which is quite true in itself and in its own sphere and extend it beyond its proper scope. If intelligence is a mere expression of nature then it would be quite right to extend that proposition to include it as well, but whether it is such an expression is the question; and this question should be answered by inference from other propositions rather than by presupposing a one-sided answer already at the start of the investigation and then deducing from it what I myself have first put into it. In short, neither of the two opinions can be justified with reasons.

Nor can an appeal to immediate consciousness settle the issue. I cannot ever become conscious either of the external forces which determine me in the system of universal necessity, nor of my own power through which I determine myself in the system of freedom. Whichever of the two opinions I may adopt, therefore, I will always adopt it simply because I happen to adopt it.

The system of freedom satisfies my heart; the opposite system kills and annihilates it. To stand there cold and dead and merely to look at the change of events an inert mirror of fleeting forms—that is an unbearable existence and I disdain and deplore it. I want to love, I want to lose myself in taking an interest, I want to be glad and be sad. For me the highest object of this interest is myself, and the only thing in me with which I can give it an ongoing content is my activity. I want to do everything for the best; want to feel glad about myslf when I have done well, and be sad about myself when I have done badly. And even this sadness is to be sweet to me, for it is interest in myself and a pledge of future improvement. Only in love is there life; without it there is death and annihilation.

But the opposite system steps up, cold and insolent, and mocks this love. If I listen to it I neither exist nor do I act. The object of my most ardent affection is a figment of my brain, demonstrably a rude deception. Instead of me there is and acts an alien force quite unknown to me; and I become quite indifferent to how it may develop. I stand there embarrassed with my heartfelt affection and with my good will; and before what I know to be the best in me, for the sake of which alone I care to exist, I blush as before a ridiculous foolishness. What is most holy to me is delivered up to mockery.

No doubt it was love of this love, interest in this interest, which, at the time before I began the investigation that now confuses me and leads me to despair, moved me unconsciously to assume my own freedom and independence. No doubt it was this interest that led me to turn an opinion, which has no more going for it than its thinkability and the unprovability of its contrary, into a conviction. And no doubt it was this interest that until now preserved me from the undertaking of wanting to explain myself and my capacity any further.

The opposite system, arid and heartless but inexhaustible in giving explanations, explains even this, my interest in freedom and my abhorrence of the opposed opinion. It explains everything that I bring up against it from my consciousness, and whenever I say that such and such is the case I am always answered in the same cool and self-assured way: I say the same thing, and in addition I'll tell you the causes which make it necessarily so. In response to all my lamenting I will say: when you speak of your heart, your love, and your interest you do so from the standpoint of immediate consciousness of yourself; and you admit this when you say that you yourself are the highest object of your interest. And on this matter it is known, and has been explicitly presented above, that this 'you' for which you show such a lively interest is, so far as it is not overt behavior, at least a *drive* of your peculiar inner nature. It is known that every drive, as surely as it is a drive, will return into itself and move itself to activity. And it is, therefore, understandable how this drive must necessarily express itself in consciousness as love for and interest in free individual activity. If you will abandon this narrow point of view of self-consciousness and adopt the highest standpoint of an overview of the universe, which after all you have promised yourself to adopt, then it will become clear to you that what you called your love is not your love but an alien love—the interest of the original force of nature in you to maintain itself as such.

And, so, do not continue to appeal to your love; for even if it could still prove something else, it would not be right even to presuppose this love here. *You don't love* yourself, for you don't even *exist;* it is *nature in you* which is interested in its own preservation. Even though there is a peculiar drive to growth and formation in a plant, you admit without dispute that the determinate activity of this drive, nevertheless, depends on forces which lie outside it. Lend this plant consciousness for a moment and it will feel its drive to grow with interest and love within itself. Persuade it with reason that this drive can do nothing of itself, but that the measure of its expression is always determined by something outside it; it will perhaps talk even as you have just talked; it will behave in a way for which a plant may be forgiven, but which would not at all be seemly in you as a higher product of nature which thinks nature as a whole.

What have I to say against this view? If I move to its territory, to the famed standpoint from which to view the universe as a whole, then without doubt I must blush and fall silent. The question is, therefore, whether I should even adopt this standpoint or whether I should remain within immediate self-consciousness, whether love should be subordinated to knowledge or knowledge to love. The latter has a bad reputation among knowledgeable people; the former makes me indescribably miserable in that it erases me myself in my being. I cannot do the latter without appearing thoughtless and foolish to myself; I cannot do the former without destroying myself.

I cannot remain undecided: my whole peace of mind and dignity depend on the answer to this question. It is just as impossible for me to decide; I simply have no sufficient reason for deciding one way or another.

Unbearable condition of uncertainty and indecision! The best and bravest decision of my life had to lead to you! What power can save me from you, what power can save me from myself?

BOOK TWO
Knowledge

Depression and dread gnawed at my insides. I cursed the appearance of day which called me to a life, the truth and meaning of which had become doubtful to me. At night I woke from disturbing dreams. Fearfully I looked for a glimmer of light to escape the aberrations of this doubt. I sought and constantly fell deeper into the labyrinth.

Once, around the hour of midnight, a wondrous shape seemed to pass before me and speak to me:

"Poor mortal," I heard it say, "you heap mistakes upon mistakes in your reasoning and think yourself wise. You tremble before specters which you yourself have worked hard to create. Have the courage to become truly wise. I bring you no new revelations. What I can teach you you already know. You only need to call it to mind now. I cannot deceive you, for you will grant me everything I say. And if you are deceived nevertheless, it will be by you. Take courage; hear me and answer my questions."

I took courage. This voice appeals to my own understanding. I will take a chance on it. It cannot think anything into me; what I am to think, I myself have to think; a conviction which I am to come to hold, I myself have to produce within me.

"Speak," I called, "whatever you may be, wondrous spirit, I will listen; ask, I will answer."

Spirit. You assume, don't you, that these objects here and those over there really are there outside of you?

I. Yes, of course.

Spirit. And how do you know that they are there?

I. I see them, I will feel them if I touch them, I can hear their sound, they manifest themselves to me through all my senses.

Spirit. So:—you may perhaps eventually take back the claim that you see and feel and hear the objects. For the present I will talk as you talk, as though by means of your seeing, feeling, etc. you really perceive objects—but only by *means* of your seeing, feeling, and the rest of your external senses. Or is it not so? Do you perceive in some way other than through your senses; and is any object present to you except so far as you see it, or feel it, etc.?

I. By no means.

Spirit. Perceivable objects, then, are present to you solely in consequence of a determination of your external sense: you know of them solely by means of your knowledge of this determination of your seeing, feeling, etc. Your statement, "There are objects outside of me" is supported by the statement, "I see, hear, feel, etc."

I. That is my view.

Spirit. Well, and how do you know that you see, hear, feel?

I. I don't understand you. Your question even seems strange.

Spirit. I'll help you understand it. Do you see your own seeing and feel your own feeling; or do you perhaps have a special, higher sense through which you perceive your external senses and their determinations?

I. Not at all. That I see and feel, and what I see and feel, I know directly and simply; I know it just because it is so, without the mediation and transmission by way of another sense. That is why your question seemed strange to me just now, because it seemed to put this immediacy of consciousness in doubt.

Spirit. That was not its intention. It was only meant to get you to make this immediacy quite clear to yourself. You have, then, an immediate consciousness of your seeing and feeling?

I. Yes.

Spirit. *Your* seeing and feeling, I say. You are, accordingly, that which sees in seeing, that which feels in feeling; and in that you are conscious of seeing are you conscious of a determination or modification *of yourself*?

I. Without doubt.

Spirit. You have an awareness of your seeing, feeling, etc., and in that way you perceive the object. Could you not also perceive it without this awareness? Could you not perhaps know an object through sight or hearing without knowing that you are seeing or hearing?

I. Not at all.

Spirit. The immediate consciousness of yourself and your determinations would therefore be the necessary condition of all other consciousness, and you know something only insofar as you know that you know this something. Nothing can occur in the latter which is not already in the former.

I. That is what I think.

Spirit. So, you only know that there are objects because you see and feel them, etc., and you know that you see and feel just because you know it, because you know it immediately. What you don't perceive immediately you don't perceive at all?

I. I see that it is so.

Spirit. In all perception you initially perceive only yourself and your own condition; and what is not contained in this perception is not perceived at all?

I. You are repeating what I have already admitted.

Spirit. And I would not tire of repeating it in every way in which it can be said if I had reason to fear that you have not yet understood it, that you have not yet indelibly impressed it upon your mind. Can you say: I am aware of external objects?

I. Definitely not, strictly speaking. For the seeing and feeling, etc., with which I take hold of things is not consciousness itself but only that of which I am first and most directly aware. Strictly speaking, I could only say: I am conscious of *my seeing or feeling things.*

Spirit. Well, then, never forget again what you have now clearly seen to be so. *In all perception you only perceive your own condition.*

But I will continue to speak your language because it is the usual one. You see, hear, feel things, you said. *How,* that is, with what properties do you see or feel them?

I. I see that object to be red, this one to be blue; I will, when I touch them, feel this one to be smooth, that one to be rough, this one cold, that one warm.

Spirit. You know therefore what that is: red, blue, smooth, rough, cold, warm?

I. Indeed I do.

Spirit. Will you not describe it to me?

I. That cannot be described. Look, direct your eye to this object; what you will perceive through the sense of sight when you see it, this I call red. Touch the surface of this other object; what you will then feel, this I call smooth. I came to this knowledge in the same way, and there is no other way of acquiring it.

Spirit. But can one not at least, once one has come to know some properties through immediate perception, derive others which are different from them by reasoning? If, e.g., someone had seen red, green, yellow, but never the color blue, or had tasted something sour, sweet, salty, but never anything bitter, could such a one not come to know, merely by thinking and comparing, what blue or bitter are, without seeing or tasting anything of the kind?

I. By no means. What is a matter of perception may only be perceived, not thought; it is not something derived, but something simply immediate.

Spirit. Remarkable. You boast of a knowledge about which you cannot tell me how you came by it. For, look, you claim to see this in the object, to feel something else, and to hear a third; you must therefore be able to distinguish seeing from feeling, and both of these from hearing?

I. Without doubt.

Spirit. You claim further to see this object to be red, that one to be blue, to feel this one to be smooth, that one rough. You must, therefore, be able to distinguish red from blue, smooth from rough?

I. Without doubt.

Spirit. Now you haven't learned this distinction by thinking and comparing these perceptions within yourself, as you have just assured me. But perhaps you have learned by the comparison of *objects outside of you* through their red or blue color, their smooth or rough surface, what you are to experience *within yourself* as red or blue, smooth or rough.

I. This is impossible; for the perception of objects has its origin in the perception of my own condition and is determined by it, and not the reverse. I first distinguish objects by distinguishing my own condition. That this particular sensation is designated by the wholly arbitrary sign 'red' and that one by the sign 'blue,' or 'smooth' or 'rough' is something I can learn; but not that and how they differ as sensations. *That* they are different I simply know by this, that I know of myself that I feel and that I feel differently in each case. *How* they are different I cannot describe; but I know that they are as different as the way I feel is different in each case; and this distinction of feelings is an immediate and in no way a learned and derived distinction.

Spirit. Which you can make independently of all knowledge of things?

I. Which I *must* make independently of it, for this knowledge itself depends upon that distinction.

Spirit. Which distinction is therefore given to you immediately through mere self-feeling?

I. Yes.

Spirit. But then you should be content to say: I feel myself affected in the manner which I call red, blue, smooth, rough. You should locate these sensations only in yourself, without transferring them to an object lying totally outside of you and purporting something to be properties of this object which after all is only your own modification.

Or tell me: when you believe that you see the object to be red or feel it to be smooth, do you perceive anything more or other than that you are affected in a certain way?

I. I have clearly seen in the preceding that indeed I perceive no more than you say; and that transference of something which is only in me onto something outside of me, from which I cannot refrain, I now find most remarkable.

I sense in myself, not in the object, for I am myself and not the object; I therefore sense only myself and my condition, and not the condition of the object. If there is a consciousness of the object, then at least it is not sensation or perception; that much is clear.

Spirit. You reason hastily. Let us consider this matter from all sides so that I can be sure that later you won't take back what you now freely admit.

Is there not something else in the object as you normally think it, something other than its red color, its smooth surface, and the like, something, in short, other than the characteristic properties which you receive through immediate sensation?

I. Yes, I think so: apart from these properties there is still the thing which has them, the bearer of the properties.

Spirit. This bearer of properties, through what sense might you perceive it? Do you see it, or do you feel it, hear it, etc., or perhaps there is a special sense for it?

I. No, I think I see it and feel it.

Spirit. Indeed? That is something we should investigate more closely! Are you ever conscious of your seeing in general, or always only of some particular instance of seeing?

I. I always have some particular visual sensation.

Spirit. And what was this particular visual sensation in respect of that object there?

I. The sensation of the color red.

Spirit. And this red is something positive, a simple sensation, a particular condition of yourself?

I. I've understood that.

Spirit. You should therefore just see this red as something simple, as a mathematical point, and surely just see it as such. At least in *you,* as your state, it obviously is just a simple determinate condition without being in any way a compound, a condition which should be found as a mathematical point. Or do you find it otherwise?

I. I have to agree with you.

Spirit. But now you spread this simple red over an extended surface which, without doubt, you *do not see,* since you *simply see red.* How might you come by this surface?

I. It is remarkable, to be sure. But I think I have found the explanation. Of course, I don't see the surface, but I *feel* it in that I run my hand over it. My visual sensation remains constantly the same during this feeling; and that is why I extend the red color over the entire surface which I *feel* while I always *see the same red.*

Spirit. It could be like that if only you felt the surface. But let's see whether this is possible. You never just feel in general, feel your feeling that is, and are now conscious of that, are you?

I. By no means. Each sensation is a particular one. One never simply sees or feels or hears, but always something determinate—a red, green, or blue color; something cold, warm, smooth, or rough; the sound of a violin; the voice of a human being and the like is seen, felt, and heard. Let's say we have agreed to that.

Spirit. Gladly. When you say you feel a surface, then what you feel immediately is only smooth or rough or the like?

I. Yes.

Spirit. And, just as in the case of the red color, this smooth or rough is something simple, a point, in you the perceiver, isn't it? And I have as much right to ask why you spread something simple which is felt over a surface, as I had to ask why you proceeded in that way with something simple which is seen.

I. This smooth surface is perhaps not equally smooth at every point, but at each one smooth to a different degree. And it may be that I lack the facility definitely to distinguish these degrees from each other, and I may lack the words with which to retain and indicate them. But I do distinguish something[1] without being aware of it, and place the things I have distinguished next to each other, and thus a surface comes to be for me.

Spirit. Can you, at the same undivided moment, have sensations opposed to each other—can you be affected in a manner containing elements which eliminate each other?

I. By no means.

Spirit. Those different degrees of smoothness which you want to assume in order to explain what you cannot explain, are they not, so far as they are different, opposed sensations which follow each other in you?

I. I can't deny that.

Spirit. You should then posit them as you actually experience them as *successive changes of the same mathematical point,* which is actually what you do on other occasions; but not as *next to each other,* as contemporaneous properties of several points in one surface.

I. I see that and find that nothing is explained by my presupposition. But my hand, with which I touch and cover the object, is itself a surface, and that is how I perceive the object as a surface; and as a surface larger than my hand, in that I can spread my hand out on it several times.

1. [Reading *'etwas'* for *'etwa.'*]

Spirit. Your hand is a surface? And how do you know that? How do you even become conscious of your hand? Is there a way other than that either you feel something else *with it,* that it is a tool, or that you feel *it itself* with another part of your body, that it is an object?

I. No, there is no other. I feel some definite thing *with* my hand, or I feel *it* with another part of my body. I do not have an immediate absolute feeling of simply my hand, any more than of my seeing or feeling in general.

Spirit. Let's for the present consider the case in which your hand is a tool, since that will be decisive for the second case as well. In the immediate awareness of your hand there can be no more in the present case than what belongs to feeling, than what presents you, and here in particular your hand, as that which touches in touching, that which feels in feeling. Now, either you feel a single thing; in which case I don't see why you spread this simple sensation over a *feeling surface* and aren't satisfied with one feeling point; or you feel different things, in which case you surely feel them *in succession* and again I don't see why you don't let these feelings follow each other in one and the same point. That your hand appears as a surface to you is just as inexplicable as that a surface appears to you at all outside of you. So please don't use the first to explain the second before you have explained the first itself. The second case in which your hand, or whichever part of your body you please, is itself the object of a feeling is easily judged by the first case. You feel this part by means of another which then is the one that feels. I raise the same questions about this latter part which I have just raised about your hand, and you will be able to answer them no more than you could answer these.

That is the case with the surface of your eyes and with every surface of your body. It may well be that the consciousness of extension outside of you derives from the consciousness of your own extension as a material body and is conditioned by it. But then you must in the first place explain this extension of your material body.

I. It is enough. I already see clearly that I neither see nor feel the extension over a surface of the properties of bodies, nor do I apprehend it through any other sense. I see that I am constantly engaged in *spreading out* what in sensation is really only a point; in putting *next to each other* what properly I should put *in succession to each other* since in pure sensation there occurs no "next to each other" but only succession. I discover that indeed I proceed just in the way in which a geometrician lets me construct his figures and extend the point into a line and the line into a surface. I wonder how I come to do that.

Spirit. You do still more and things still more wonderful. This surface which you assume on this body you can, of course, neither see nor feel nor perceive through any sense at all, but one can surely say in a certain context that you see the red color and feel the smooth texture *on it.* But you yourself continue this surface and extend it into a mathematical body, as you have just admitted to extending a line into a surface. You further assume an existing interior of the body behind its surface. Tell me, can you see or feel anything behind this surface or perceive it through any other sense?

I. By no means. The space behind the surface is invisible and intangible to me and perceptible by none of my senses.

Spirit. And nevertheless you assume such an interior which you simply don't perceive.

I. I admit it and my astonishment increases.

Spirit. What is it then which you think is behind its surface?

I. Well, I think something similar to the surface, something perceptible.

Spirit. We must be definite about this. Can you divide the mass which makes up this body for you?

I. I can divide it infinitely; not with instruments, of course, but in thought. No possible part is the smallest, so that it could not be further divided.

Spirit. Will you, in this dividing, come to a part which you think will in itself no longer be perceptible, not visible, not tangible, etc.— in itself, I say, even if it might no longer be perceptible to your sense organs?

I. By no means.

Spirit. Visible, tangible in general? Or with a definite property, color, smoothness or roughness, or the like?

I. In the latter way. There is nothing visible or tangible in general because there is no seeing or feeling in general.

Spirit. You therefore spread sensibility throughout the entire mass, your own familiar sensibility, visibility as colored, tangibility as rough or smooth, etc.; and this mass is everywhere nothing other than the sensible itself. Or do you disagree?

I. Not at all. What you say follows from what I have just seen to be so and have admitted to you.

Spirit. And still you don't really perceive anything behind the surface, and have perceived nothing behind it.

I. When I penetrate it I will perceive.

Spirit. You know that in advance, then. And you have never carried out the division to infinity in which you claim never to be able to come upon something simply unperceivable, have you, nor can you carry it out?

I. I cannot carry it out.

Spirit. To a perception which you have had then, you add in thought another one which you have not had?

I. I only perceive what I attribute to the surface; I do not perceive what lies behind it, and yet I assume that something perceivable is there as well. Yes, you are right.

Spirit. The actual perception agrees in part with what you predicted about it in advance?

I. When I penetrate the surface of the body I indeed find something perceptible behind it as I predicted. Yes, you are right about that as well.

Spirit. In part, however, you assert something about perception which could occur in no actual perception.

I. I assert that in a division of the physical mass to infinity I would never come upon a part which would in itself be imperceptible, since I am satisfied that I cannot divide the mass to infinity. Yes, you are right about that as well.

Spirit. So, nothing remains in your object other than something perceptible—a property. This perceptible something you extend through a continuous, infinitely divisible space, and the true support of the properties of the thing which you sought would therefore be the space which it occupies?

I. Nevertheless, I am not content with this but feel that apart from this perceptible something and this space there is still something else to be thought in this object. But I cannot demonstrate this other thing to you and must therefore admit to you that so far I have found no other support than space itself.

Spirit. Do admit, however, what now you see to be so. The remaining obscurities will gradually clear up and you will become acquainted with what you do not yet know. But space itself is not perceived, and you don't understand how you come by a conception of it and how you come to extend sensible things through it?

I. That's true.

Spirit. Just as little do you understand how you even come by the supposition of sensible things outside of you since you only perceive your own sensation in you, not as the property of a thing but as an affection of yourself?

I. That's true. I clearly see that I perceive only myself, simply my own condition, but not the object; that I do not see it, feel it, hear it, etc., but rather that just there, where there should be an object, all seeing, feeling, etc., comes to an end.

But I have a hunch. Sensations as affections of myself are nothing extended but something simple. And different sensations are not *next* to each other in space, but follow *after* each other in time. But nevertheless I extend them throughout a space. How would it be if just through this extension and immediately with it, that which properly is only sensation were transformed for me into *something* sensible, and if it were just this point from which came the consciousness of an object outside of me?

Spirit. Your hunch may prove correct. But even if we could directly promote it to a conviction it would still not give us complete insight because the higher question would always remain: how do you come to extend your sensation through a space in the first place? Let us therefore straightway tackle this question; and let us take hold of it (I have my reasons for this) more generally in the following way: how do you at all come to move outside yourself with your consciousness, which after all is immediately only a consciousness of yourself, and add to the sensation which you perceive, something sensed and sensible which you do not perceive?

I. Sweet or bitter, as well as ill-scented or fragrant, rough or smooth, cold or warm, signify, when considered as properties of a thing, that which excites such a taste and smell and feeling in me. The same is true of sounds. A relation to me is always indicated, and it would never occur to me that the sweet or bitter taste, the fragrance or the bad smell, etc., could be in the thing; it is in me and in my opinion is merely excited by the thing. It may seem to be otherwise with sensations of sight, with colors, which may not be pure sensations but something intermediate. But when I think about it carefully, then red and the like also refer to what produces a particular sensation of sight in me. And this leads me to understand how I might at all come by a thing outside of me. I am affected, I simply know that: this my affection must have a cause: this cause does not lie in me, therefore it is outside of me. That is how I reason quickly without being aware of it and posit such a cause, *the object*. The cause must be such that just this particular affection can be explained by it. I am affected in a manner which I call a sweet taste; the object must therefore be of a kind that excites a sweet taste or, with abbreviation of language, it must itself be sweet. In this way I arrive at the *determination* of the object.

Spirit. There may be some truth in what you say, even though it is not the whole truth on the subject. We will doubtless find out more about this in due time. Since, however, in other cases you indisputably think according to the principle of causality—I will call the assertion you just made that something, in this case your affection, must have a cause, the principle of causality—since in other cases, I say, you indisputably think according to this principle, it cannot be superfluous to consider this procedure in detail and to become quite clear about what in fact you do when you make use of it. Let us assume for the time being that your explanation is completely correct and that by unnoticed inference from the effect to a cause you first come to the supposition of a thing. What were you conscious of as your perception?

I. That I was affected in a particular way.

Spirit. But you were not conscious of a thing which affects you, at least not as a perception?

I. By no means. I have already admitted that.

Spirit. By means of the principle of causality, then, you add to a knowledge which you have, another knowledge which you do not have?

I. You express yourself strangely.

Spirit. Perhaps I'll be able to remove that strangeness. Incidentally, take my expressions to mean what they may to you. They are only to guide you in producing the same thought in yourself as I have produced in me, not to function as a precept for you on how to talk. Once you have grasped the thought firmly and clearly, then express it as you please and with as much variety as you please. You may be sure that you will always express it well.

How and through what do you know of the affection of yourself?

I. It is hard to put my answer into words: Because my consciousness as subjective, as determination of me so far as I am an intelligence, is immediately concerned with this affection as that of which it is *conscious* and with which it is inseparably united; because I am conscious at all only so far as I know of such an affection; know of *it*, just as I know of myself.

Spirit. You have then an organ as it were, consciousness itself, with which you grasp your affection?

I. Yes.

Spirit. But an organ with which you grasp the object you do *not* have?

I. Since you have persuaded me that I neither see nor feel the object nor grasp it through any external sense whatever, I find myself forced to admit that I have no such organ.

Spirit. Consider this carefully. It might be held against you that you admit this to me. What after all is your external sense, and how can you call it external if it does not relate to external objects and is the organ for them?

I. I want truth and care little for what will be held against me. I *distinguish* simply because I distinguish green, sweet, red, smooth, bitter, fragrance, rough, the sound of a violin, bad smell, the sound of a trumpet. Among these sensations I posit some in a certain respect as simply *similar*, as in another respect I simply distinguish them; so I perceive green and red as similar, sweet and bitter as similar, smooth and rough as similar, etc., and this similarity I perceive as seeing, tasting, feeling, etc. Seeing, tasting, etc., are not themselves real perceptions, for I never simply see or taste, as you have already noted earlier, but always see red or green, etc., always taste sweet or bitter, etc. Seeing, tasting, and the like are only *higher determinations of real sensations;* they are classes under which I classify sensations, though not deliberately but guided by immediate sensation itself. Therefore I do not see any *external senses* in them anywhere, but only *particular determinations of the object of the inner sense,* of my affections. How they come to be external senses for me, or more exactly how I come to take them to be such and designate them as such, that is just now the question. I do not take back my admission that I have no organ for the object.

Spirit. And yet you talk of objects as though you really knew about them and had an organ for the knowledge of them.

I. Yes.

Spirit. And you do this, according to your earlier assumption, *in consequence of the knowledge which you really have,* and for which you have an organ, and for the sake of this knowledge.

I. That's how it is.

Spirit. Your actual knowledge—the knowledge of your affections—is to you an incomplete knowledge as it were, which according to your claim has to be supplemented with another knowledge. This other new knowledge you think of, you describe, not as one you have, for you have it by no means, but as one which you really should still have in addition to the knowledge you actually have, and which you would have if you had an organ for it. It is as though you said: "Admittedly I know nothing about things; but surely there must be things and if only I could find them then there would be no problem about them." You think of another organ, which of course you don't have, and you relate it to things, you grasp them with it—always only in thought, of course. Strictly speaking you have no *consciousness of things,* but only *a consciousness* (produced by going beyond your actual consciousness by means of the principle of causality) *of a consciousness of things* (which are supposed to exist and be necessary, but which are inaccessible to you). And now you will realize that according to your assumption you add to the knowledge which you do have another knowledge which you do not have.

I. I must admit it.

Spirit. Let us then from now on call this second knowledge which is assumed in consequence of another knowledge, let us call this second knowledge a *mediated* knowledge, and the first one an *immediate* knowledge. A certain school calls the procedure we have just described, so far as we have managed to describe it, a synthesis. By this term you should, at least here, understand not a *connection* of two items which already existed prior to this connecting, but an *attaching,* an addition of a quite new item which first comes to be in this attaching to another which exists quite independent of it.

So, the first consciousness you find there already, just as you find yourself, and you don't find yourself without it; the second you first produce only in consequence of the first.

I. But not *after* the first in time; for I am conscious of the thing in the same undivided moment as I become aware of myself.

Spirit. I'm not speaking of such a sequence at all. Rather, I think that if subsequently you think about this undivided consciousness of yourself and the thing, distinguish them and inquire into their relation, you will find that the latter is conditioned by the former— that is, only if you presuppose the former can you conceive the latter as possible, but not the reverse.

I. So it seems to me. If that is all you meant to say then I agree with your claim and have already agreed with it.

Spirit. You *produce*, I say, the second consciousness: you bring it forth by means of a real act of your mind. Or does it seem otherwise to you?

I. I have, of course, indirectly already admitted this as well. To the consciousness which I find as I find myself I add another one which I do not find in myself at all; I extend and as it were double my actual consciousness, and that is, of course, an act. But I am tempted to take back either my admission or my whole presupposition. For I am well aware of the acts of my mind as such: I know it when I form a general concept or when in doubtful cases I choose one of the possible ways of behaving which are open to me. But I am in no way aware of the act by which you claim that I produce the presentation of an object outside me.

Spirit. Don't let that confuse you. You only become aware of the acts of your mind so far as you go through a condition of indefiniteness and indecision of which you are also aware and which those acts put an end to. Such indecision does not occur in our case: the mind does not first need to consider which object it is to add to its particular sensation. This occurs of itself. There are terms in the language of philosophy with which to make a distinction here. A mental act of which we become conscious as such is called *freedom.* An act without consciousness of acting, pure *spontaneity.* Please notice that I by no means ascribe to you an immediate consciousness of the act as such, but only this: that when you think about it afterwards you find that it must be an act. The higher question about what it may be that does not allow such indecision and consciousness of our acting to occur, will doubtless be resolved of itself later on.

This act of your mind is called *thinking,* which word I have also used so far with your agreement. And one says that thinking occurs spontaneously, to distinguish it from sensation, which is mere receptivity. *How,* then, given your earlier assumption, do you come to add in thought an object, about which you know nothing, to your sensation, which of course you do have?

I. My sensation must have a cause: this I assume and then reason from there.

Spirit. Won't you tell me at the outset what you mean by a cause?

I. I find something to be determinate in such and such a way. I cannot be satisfied with knowing that it *is* so, and I assume that it has *become* so, and that not through itself but through an outside force. This outside force which made it so *contains* the cause, and the expression through which it made it so *is* the cause of this determination of the thing. That my sensation has a cause means that it is produced in me by an outside force.

Spirit. This outside force you now add in thought to your sensation of which you are immediately conscious and that is how the presentation of an object comes to be for you? Let it be so.

Now please take note: *if* the sensation must have a cause then I will admit the correctness of your inference, and agree that you are fully justified in assuming objects outside of you even though you neither know nor can know anything about them. But how do you know and how do you propose to prove to me *that* it must have a cause? Or, expressed with the generality of the above principle of yours; why can you not be satisfied to know that something *is* so; why do you assume that it *became* so; or, if I were willing to overlook that, that it became so *through an outside force.* I notice that you always only assume this.

I. I admit it. But in fact I cannot think otherwise. It seems that I know it immediately.

Spirit. What this answer, that you know it immediately, could mean we will see if we should come back to it as the only possible one. For the present let's first try all other possible ways of deriving that claim that something must have a cause.

Do you perhaps know it by immediate perception?

I. How could I, since all that is ever contained in perception is that something *is* in me, actually how I am determined; but never that it has *become,* much less that it has come to be through an alien force lying outside all perception?

Spirit. Or is it a principle which you have formulated through observation of things outside of you whose cause you always find outside of them, and which you have elevated to universality, and now also apply to yourself and your condition?

I. Don't treat me like a child and think me capable of patent absurdities. Through the principle of causality I first arrive at things outside of me; how could I then first have arrived at this principle through these things outside of me? Does the earth rest on the great elephant, and the great elephant again on the earth?

Spirit. Or perhaps that principle is derived from another general truth?

I. Which again could be justified neither by immediate perception nor by the observation of external things, and about the origin of which you would once again ask questions? This assumed fundamental truth I could also only know immediately. It would be better for me to say that straightway about the principle of causality and to remain undecided about your conjecture.

Spirit. So be it: apart from the first immediate knowledge through sensation of our condition we have then obtained in addition a second immediate knowledge which aims at general truths.

I. So it seems.

Spirit. The particular knowledge which is here at issue, i.e., that your affections must have a cause, is completely independent of the knowledge of things?

I. Of course. This latter knowledge is itself first made possible by the former.

Spirit. And you simply have it in yourself?

I. Yes, I simply have it; for only by means of it do I go beyond myself.

Spirit. From yourself and through yourself and through your immediate knowledge you therefore prescribe laws to being and its interrelations?

I. On careful reflection, I only prescribe laws to my presentations of being and its interconnections, and it would be more careful to choose that expression.

Spirit. So be it. Now, do you become aware of this law in any other way than by proceeding in accordance with it ?

I. My consciousness begins with the sensation of my condition;

immediately with that I connect the presentation of an object according to the law of causality; both the consciousness of my condition and the presentation of an object are indivisibly united. There is no consciousness *between them,* and *before* this one indivisible consciousness there is no other consciousness. No, it is impossible that I become aware of this law before or in any other way than by proceeding in accordance with it.

Spirit. So you proceed in accordance with it without being particularly aware of it; you immediately and simply proceed in accordance with it. But just now you were aware of it and expressed it as a general principle. How might you come by this particular awareness?

I. Without doubt as follows: I observe myself later and realize that I proceed that way, and formulate what is common in my procedure as a general principle.

Spirit. You can then become conscious of your procedure?

I. Without doubt. I can guess the intention of your questions; here is the second kind of immediate consciousness mentioned above, that of *my activity,* just as sensation is the first kind, the consciousness of *my passivity.*

Spirit. Right. You *can,* I said, become aware of your procedure afterwards through free observation of yourself and reflecting on yourself; but you do not have to become conscious of it; you do not become immediately conscious of activity merely insofar as you inwardly act?

I. Yet I must originally be conscious of it, for after all I am immediately conscious of the presentation of the object at the same time as the sensation. I have found the solution: I become immediately conscious of my activity, but not *as such.* Rather it appears to me as *a given.* This consciousness is consciousness of the object. Afterwards, through free reflection, I can also become aware of it as an activity.

My immediate consciousness is composed of two constituent parts, the consciousness of my passivity, the sensation; and the consciousness of my activity, in the production of an object according to the principle of causality; which latter is immediately annexed to the first. Consciousness of *the object* is only a *consciousness of my production of a presentation of the object,* which is not recognized as such. About this production I know simply because I am the one

who is doing the producing. And so all consciousness is only immediate consciousness, a consciousness of myself, and is now fully
intelligible. Do I reason correctly?

Spirit. Incomparably. But what accounts for the necessity and
universality with which you affirm your principles, such as here the
principle of causality?

I. The immediate feeling that I cannot proceed otherwise, as
surely as I have reason, and that no rational being other than
myself can proceed otherwise, as surely as it is a rational being.
That everything accidental, such as my affection in the present
case, *has* a cause means: *I have always in thought added a cause, and
everyone, if he is to think at all, will similarly* feel compelled in thought
to add a cause.

Spirit. You realize then that all knowledge is only knowledge of
yourself, that your consciousness never goes beyond yourself, and
that what you take to be a consciousness of the object is nothing but
a consciousness of your *positing of an object* which, in accordance
with an inner law of your thought, you necessarily engage in together with sensation.

I. Just continue boldly with your reasoning. I didn't want to disturb you and even helped to develop the intended conclusions. But
seriously now: I take back my whole presupposition, namely, that
by means of the principle of causality I arrive at things outside of
me; and inwardly I had taken it back as soon as with it we came
upon something which is patently incorrect.

For in this way I would also become conscious of a mere *force*
outside of me, and of this force as something merely *thought;* as,
for example, to explain magnetic phenomena I think a magnetic
force in nature, and to explain electrical phenomena I think an
electrical one.

My world, however, does not appear to me as such a mere
thought, the thought of a mere force. It is something extended;
something through and through sensible, not just through its expression like a force, but in itself; it does not, like a force, produce
properties—rather, it *has* properties; inwardly I am conscious of my
awareness of it in quite another way than I am conscious of mere
thinking; *it appears to me as perception,* not withstanding that it is

proved not to be perception and that it would be difficult for me to describe this kind of consciousness and to distinguish it from other kinds.

Spirit. Nevertheless, you must attempt such a description. Without it I do not understand you and we will never come to clarity.

I. I'll try to clear the way for it. I beg you, spirit, if your sense organ is like mine, then fix your eye on the red object there before us, and impartially submit to the impression and in the meantime forget your arguments; and now tell me sincerely what is going on in you.

Spirit. I can completely enter into the operation of your sense organ; and it is not for me to deny any impression which is actually there. Just tell me what should be going on in me.

I. Do you not immediately and at a single glance see and take in the surface, I say *the surface;* does it not at once stand before you completely? Are you conscious in even the remotest and most obscure way of this extending of a simple red point into a line, and of this line into a surface, of which you spoke above? You only divide this surface afterwards and think of points and lines on it. Would you not, and would not everyone who observes himself without prejudice independent of your above arguments assert and insist that he really *sees* a surface, a surface of such and such a color?

Spirit. I grant you everything, and what I find in self-observation is just as you describe it.

But, to begin with, you have not forgotten, have you, that it is not our intention to tell each other what takes place in consciousness as in a newspaper of the human mind; but to think the different mental events in relation to each other, and to explain one by another and to derive one from the other: that therefore none of your observations, which of course must not be denied but explained, can upset any of my correct arguments?

I. I will never lose sight of that.

Spirit. Then don't let the remarkable similarity between real perception and this consciousness of bodies outside of you that you cannot describe yet, make you overlook the great difference which exists after all between the two.

I. I was just about to indicate the difference. True, both appear as immediate consciousness, not learned or produced. But sensation is consciousness of *my condition*. Not so consciousness of the object, in which initially there simply is no relation to me. I know that it *is* and leave it at that; it does not concern me. If in the first I appear to myself as soft clay which sometimes is formed, squeezed, and pressed in one way and sometimes in another, then in the second I appear to myself as a mirror before which the objects simply pass without it itself being in the slightest changed by that.

But this difference speaks in my favor. I seem all the more, really, to have a particular consciousness of an existence (I say *existence*) outside of me, a consciousness quite independent of the sensation of my condition, since this latter also differs in kind from the former.

Spirit. You observe well; but just don't be too hasty in drawing conclusions.

If what we agreed to above remains true, and you can immediately be conscious only of yourself, and if the consciousness at issue now is not a consciousness of your passivity and is not to be a consciousness of your activity, might it then not be a consciousness of your own *existence* which is just not recognized as such? Your existence so far as you *know* or are an intelligence?

I. I don't understand you. But help me out, because I would like to understand.

Spirit. I must ask you to pay very close attention, for I am compelled to go deeper here than ever and to consider widely.

What are you?

I. To answer your question in the most general way: I am I, I myself.

Spirit. I am quite satisfied with that answer. What does that mean when you say 'I,' what is contained in that concept, and how do you come by it?

I. I can only clarify that by contrast. *The thing* is supposed to be something outside of me, the knower. *I* am the knower himself, one with the knower. About the consciousness of the first the question arises: since the thing does not know about itself, how can a knowledge of the thing come to be; since I am not the thing myself, nor any of its determinations since all its determinations fall completely within the sphere of its being and in no way within the sphere of my being, how can a consciousness of the thing come to be *in me*? How does the thing get inside me? What is the connection between the subject, me, and the object of my knowledge, the thing? This question does not arise about *me*. I have knowledge in myself, for I am intelligence. What I am, thereof I *know*, because I am it. And that which I know immediately simply by existing, that is *me*, because I immediately know about it. Here no connection between subject and object is required; my own being is this connection. I am subject and object: and this subject-objectivity, this return of knowledge into itself, is what I designate with the concept 'I,' if I think anything definite at all with this concept.

Spirit. So, the identity of subject and object would be your essence as intelligence?

I. Yes.

Spirit. Now, can you grasp, can you become conscious of this identity, of that which is neither subject nor object but which is the foundation of both and out of which these two first come to be?

I. By no means. I am always conscious only on condition that *that which is conscious* and *that of which there is consciousness* appear distinct from each other. I cannot even conceive of a different consciousness. In finding myself I find myself as subject *and* object, which two however are immediately connected.

Spirit. Can you become conscious of the moment in which this incomprehensible one separates into these two?

I. How could I, since my consciousness first becomes possible with and through their separation, since it is my consciousness itself which separates them? But beyond that consciousness there is no consciousness.

Spirit. This separation, therefore, would be what you necessarily find in yourself as you become conscious of yourself? *It* would properly be your original being?

I. That's how it is.

Spirit. And where would it have its foundation?

I. I am intelligence and have consciousness in myself. That separation is the condition, it is the result of consciousness as such. It therefore has its foundation in myself, like consciousness.

Spirit. You are intelligence, you said. At least that is all that is at issue here. And as such you become object for yourself. Your knowing, as objective, is therefore placed before you, before your knowing as subjective, and is present to this; of course without your being able to become conscious of this placing.

I. That's true.

Spirit. Can you not add something toward the more exact characterization of the subjective and the objective, such as how they appear in consciousness?

I. The subjective appears as containing within itself the foundation of a consciousness in respect of *form,* but not at all in respect of the determinate content. That there is a consciousness, an inner looking and shaping—of that the foundation is in the subjective itself; that *just this* is seen is something for which it depends on the objective, on which it is fixed, and by which it is, as it were, swept away. The objective on the other hand contains the foundation of its being within itself. It is in and for itself, it is as it is because it just happens to be so. The subjective appears as the passive unmoving mirror of the objective; the latter is present to the former. The reason why the subjective mirrors lies in it itself. The reason why just this and nothing else is mirrored lies in the objective.

Spirit. The subjective as such, according to its inner nature, would accordingly be constituted just as above you described in particular the consciousness of existing things outside of you?

I. True, and this agreement is remarkable. I'm beginning to find it halfway plausible that the presentation of a being outside of and independent of me could come from the inner laws of my consciousness itself, and that this presentation might at bottom be nothing other than the presentation of these laws themselves.

Spirit. Why only halfway?

I. Because I do not yet understand why it would turn out to be just *such* a presentation, in respect of its content, a presentation of a mass extended in continuous space.

Spirit. That it is only your sensation which you extend in space you have already recognized above; and you suspected that your sensation might turn into something sensible just by its extension in space. At present, therefore, we need concern ourselves only with space itself and need only explain its generation from bare consciousness.

I. Yes.

Spirit. Then let us make the attempt. I know that you cannot become conscious of your intelligent activity as such, so far as it remains *originally and invariably fixed upon one thing.* You cannot become conscious of your activity in this condition, which begins when the activity begins to exist and which cannot be removed without removing the activity along with it, and I will therefore not suppose such a consciousness in you. But you can become conscious of it insofar as within the invariable condition it moves *from one variable condition* to *another variable one.* If now you observe it under these circumstances, how does it appear to you, this inner agility of your mind?

I. My mental capacity seems inwardly to move back and forth, quickly to move from one to the other; in short, it appears to me as a *drawing of a line.* A determinate thought is a point on this line.

Spirit. And why just as a drawing of a line?

I. Am I to give reasons for something whose confines I cannot transgress without stepping out of my own existence? It simply is so.

Spirit. This, then, is how a *particular* act of your consciousness appears to you. And in what image will your knowledge in general appear to you, *knowledge which is not produced but innate,* knowledge of which all particular thinking is only the revival and further determination?

I. Evidently as one in which one can draw lines and make points in all directions: that is, as *space.*

Spirit. And now it will be fully clear to you how something which proceeds from yourself could appear to you as being outside of you, how it even must necessarily so appear.

You have penetrated to the true source of the presentations of things outside of you. This presentation is not perception; you only perceive yourself. And just as little is it thought; things don't appear to you as something merely thought. It really is consciousness of being outside of you, and indeed absolutely immediate consciousness of such being, just as perception is immediate consciousness of your condition. Don't let sophists and half philosophers dumbfound you: things don't appear to you through a representative; of the thing which is there and can be there you become immediately conscious; and there is no thing other than the one you become conscious of. You yourself are this thing; you are placed before yourself and projected out of yourself by the inmost ground of your being, your finitude; and everything you see outside of you is always you yourself. This consciousness has quite appropriately been called *intuition.* In all consciousness I intuit myself; for I am I:

for the subjective, that which is conscious, it is *in*tuition. And the objective, that which is intuited and of which there is consciousness, I am also myself, the same I which is also the intuiting one, but only objectively, appearing before the subjective. In this respect consciousness is an active looking-*at* that which I intuit, a looking-out of myself out of myself: a carrying-out of myself out of myself by the only kind of acting which is proper to me, by looking. I am a living seeing. I see (consciousness), and see my seeing (that of which I'm conscious).

That too is why the thing is entirely transparent to the eye of your mind, because it is your mind itself. You divide, you limit, you determine the possible forms of things and the relations of these forms of all perception in advance. No wonder; by doing that you always only limit and determine your knowledge itself of which you know without doubt. That is why a knowledge of things becomes possible. It is not in the thing and does not flow out from it. It flows out from you while it exists and it is your own being.

There is no external sense for there is no external perception. There is, however, an external intuition, not of the *thing*, but this external intuition (this *knowledge* which is external to the subjective and appears to it as appearing before it) is itself the thing and there is no other. Through this external intuition even perception and the senses are seen as external. It will always be true since it has been proved: I never[2] see or feel the surface, but I intuit my seeing or feeling as seeing or feeling a surface. Illuminated, transparent, unobstructed, and penetrable space, the purest image of my knowledge, is not seen but intuited, and *in it my seeing itself* is intuited. Light is not outside of me but in me, and I myself am light. Above you answered my question about how you know of your seeing, feeling, etc., and in general about your sensation by saying that you knew of it immediately. Now you will perhaps be able to give me a more detailed account of this immediate consciousness of your sensation.

I. It must be a double one. Sensation is itself an immediate consciousness: I *sense* my sensation. This in no way gives me any knowledge of being, but only *the feeling of my own condition*. But I do not

---

2. [Reading *'nimmer'* for *'immer.'*]

originally only sense but I also intuit; for I am not only a practical being but also intelligence. I also *intuit* my sensing; and this is how I get *the knowledge of being* out of myself and my being. *Sensation* is transformed into *something sensible;* my affection, red, smooth, and the like into *something red, smooth,* etc., outside of me which (and the sensation of which) I intuit in space because my intuition itself is space. This also makes clear why I believe I see or feel surfaces which in fact I neither see nor feel. I only intuit my seeing or feeling as seeing or feeling a surface.

Spirit. You have understood me, or actually yourself, very well.

I. But then the thing does not at all come to be for me, either noticed or unnoticed, through an inference based on the principle of causality; rather it immediately arises for my consciousness and simply stands before it without any inference at all. I cannot say, as I did just now, that sensation is transformed into something sensible. The sensible, as such, is what is first in consciousness. Consciousness does not begin with an affection such as red, smooth, and the like, but with something red, smooth, etc., outside of me.

Spirit. But if you now had to explain to me what red, smooth, and the like are, would you be able to say anything other than that they are what affects you in a certain way which you call red, smooth, and the like?

I. I may well not—if you ask me, and if I address myself to your question at all and make an attempt to explain. But originally no one asks me, and I don't ask myself. I quite forget myself and lose myself in intuition; I don't at all become aware of my condition but only of a being outside of me. Red, green, and the like are properties of the object. It just is red or green and that is that. It is not explained any further; no more than, as in our earlier agreement, red or green taken as affection can be explained any further. This is most easily noticed in visual sensation. Color appears outside of me, and human understanding left to itself without further thought about itself would hardly come to explain red or green as that which excites a particular affection in it.

Spirit. You would no doubt say the same of sweet or sour? This is not the place to inquire whether the impressions of sight are pure sensation, or whether they aren't rather something halfway between sensation and intuition and the means of connecting the two in our minds. But I fully admit your observation and heartily welcome it. You can of course disappear from your own awareness in intuition; and if you don't particularly pay attention to yourself and have no interest in some external action or other, you will even naturally and necessarily disappear from your own awareness. This is the observation to which the defenders of a purported consciousness of things existing in themselves outside of us appeal if one shows them that the principle of causality, through which one could infer such things, is only in us. They then deny that there is any inference at all, and one should not object to this denial of theirs so far as they are talking of actual consciousness in certain cases. These are the same defenders who, if one explains the nature of intuition to them with the laws of their own intelligence, themselves again fall back on inference and do not tire of repeating that there must be something outside of us which makes us have just the presentations we have.

I. Don't get wrought up over these people now, but teach me. I have no preconceived opinion but want first to look for the true opinion.

Spirit. Nevertheless intuition necessarily proceeds from the perception of your own condition. Only you are not always clearly conscious of this perception as you have seen above through inferences. Also, even in that consciousness in which you lose yourself in the object, there is always something that is only possible through an unnoticed thinking of yourself and a close observation of your own condition.

I. So that constantly and under all circumstances my consciousness of things outside of me is accompanied by an unnoticed consciousness of myself?

Spirit. Quite so.

I. The former is determined by the latter to be as it is?

Spirit. That's what I mean.

I. Show me that and I'll be satisfied.

Spirit. Do you posit things only in space or do you posit each thing as filling a definite part of space?

I. The latter. Each thing has its definite size.

Spirit. And the different things, do they fall into the same parts of space?

I. By no means. They exclude each other. They are next to each other, above and below, behind and in front of each other, closer to me or more distant.

Spirit. And how do you come to this measuring and ordering of things in space? Is it sensation?

I. How could it be, since space itself is no sensation?

Spirit. Or intuition?

I. This cannot be. Intuition is immediate and infallible. What is given in intuition does not appear as having been brought forth and cannot deceive. But I even catch myself estimating, measuring, and considering as seems right to me the size of an object, its distance, its position in relation to other objects; and every beginner is familiar with the observation that originally we see objects next to each other in the same line, that we must first learn to estimate their greater distance or proximity, that children reach for distant objects as though they lay just before their eyes, and that people who are born blind would do the same were they suddenly to receive sight. That presentation is therefore a judgment; not an intuition but an ordering of my manifold intuitions by the understanding. Also, in this estimating of size, distance, etc., I can err; and the so-called visual illusions don't seem to be deceptions of sight at all but erroneous judgments about the size of the object, about the size of its parts in relation to each other, and what follows from that about its true shape and about its distance from me and other objects. It really is in space as I intuit it, and the color which I see on it I also really see. In that there is no deception.

Spirit. And what might be the principle of this judging? Let's take the most definite and easiest case, that of judging the proximity or distance of objects from you. By what might you estimate this distance?

I. Without doubt by the greater strength or weakness of otherwise similar impressions. I see before me two objects of the same red. The one whose color I see more clearly is closer to me; the one whose color I perceive more weakly is more distant, more distant in proportion as I see the color more weakly.

Spirit. You judge distance then according to the measure of strength or weakness. And how do you judge this strength or weakness itself?

I. Evidently only so far as I pay attention to my affections as such and, in addition, to a very subtle difference in them. You have

defeated me. All consciousness of objects outside of me is determined by the clear and exact consciousness of my own condition,
and in that there is always an inference from the effect in me to a
cause outside of me.

Spirit. You give up easily, and now I will myself have to continue
the argument against me in your place. Surely, my proof only applies to cases in which there is an actual estimating and considering
of the size, the distance and the position of the object, and in which
you become conscious of this procedure. But you will admit that
this is not usually the case, that rather in most cases you become
aware of an object's size, distance, etc., immediately at the same
undivided moment in which you become aware of the object.

I. When the distance of the object is judged only by the strength
of the impression then this quick judgment is merely a consequence of the earlier estimating. Through lifelong practice I have
learned quickly to notice the strength of the impression and to
judge the distance accordingly. It is a combination of sensation,
intuition, and past judgment which I had already worked to put
together in the past, a combination from which my present presentation proceeds. And I become conscious only of this presentation.
I no longer apprehend just red, green, or the like, outside of me,
but red or green *at such and such a distance.* This last addition,
however, is a *mere renewal of a judgment already produced earlier by
deliberation.*

Spirit. Didn't it become clear to you at the same time whether you
intuit the thing outside of you, or whether you think it, or whether
you do both and to what extent each of the two?

I. Completely. And I believe that I have now attained the most
complete insight into the generation of a presentation of an object
outside of me.

1. Because I am I, I am aware of myself, and that partly as a
   practical being and partly as an intelligence. The first consciousness is *sensation,* and the second is *intuition,* unlimited
   space.
2. I cannot apprehend something unlimited, for I am limited.
   Therefore, through thought, I limit a certain space in space in
   general and place the first in a certain relation with the last.
3. The standard by which I measure this limited space is the measure of my own sensation; according to the principle which one
   might formulate and express perhaps as follows: what affects me

to such and such a degree is to be placed in space in such and
such a relation with the rest of what affects me.

The *property* of the thing has its origin in the sensation of my own
condition, and *space*, which it fills, has its origin in intuition. The
two are connected by thought; the first is transferred to the second.
What we said above is, of course, true: by being placed into space,
that which properly is only my condition becomes a property of the
thing for me. But it is placed in space, not by intuition but by
thought, by *measuring* and *ordering* thought. In this act there is,
however, no thinking up, no creating by thought, but merely a
determination of what is given in sensation and intuition independently of thought.

Spirit. What affects me to such and such a degree is to be placed
in such and such a relation. This is how you reason when you limit
and order the objects in space. Now, does not the claim that something affects you to a certain degree rest on the assumption that it
affects you at all?

I. Without doubt.

Spirit. And is it possible to have any conception at all of an external object which is not limited and ordered in space in this way?

I. No; no object is just in space, but always in some definite space.

Spirit. Accordingly, whether you now become aware of it or not,
every external object is conceived as affecting you; and as surely as
it is conceived it is conceived as taking up a definite space.

I. That follows.

Spirit. And what kind of a conception is the conception of something affecting you?

I. Evidently a kind of thinking. In particular a thinking according
to the principle of causality mentioned above. Now I see still more
clearly that the consciousness of an object is as it were attached to
my self-consciousness in two ways, partly through intuition and
partly through thinking according to the principle of causality. As
strange as this may seem, the object is both the immediate object of
my consciousness and it is inferred.

Spirit. But each in a different respect, I suppose. Surely it must be
possible for you to become conscious of this thinking of the object?

I. Without doubt. Even though I don't usually become conscious
of it.

Spirit. To the passivity in you, your affection, you add in thought an activity outside of you, as you earlier described thinking according to the principle of causality?

I. Yes.

Spirit. And with the same meaning and validity as you described it above. You just happen to think in this way and have to think in this way. You cannot change it and can know nothing more than that you think this way?

I. Yes. We've already worked all this out in general.

Spirit. You think *up* the object, I said: so far as it is something thought it is a product merely of your thinking?

I. Yes, of course; for that follows from what was said above.

Spirit. And what is this thought-up object, this object inferred according to the principle of causality?

I. A *force* outside of me.

Spirit. Which you neither sense nor intuit?

I. Not at all. I am always well aware that I simply do not apprehend it immediately but only by means of its expressions, even though I ascribe to it an existence independent of me. I think that I am affected. There must therefore be something which affects me.

Spirit. This would, of course, make the intuited thing and the thought thing two very different things. That which really does immediately appear before you extended in space is the *intuited* thing. The inner force in it which does not appear to you at all, but the existence of which you assert only through an inference, is the *thought* thing.

I. The inner force in it, you said, and it occurs to me now that you are right. I place this force into space myself as well; I transfer it to the intuited mass which occupies space.

Spirit. And how, according to your necessary view, are this force and this mass to relate to each other?

I. In the following way: the mass and its properties are themselves the effect and expression of the inner force. This force has two effects. One through which it maintains itself and gives itself this particular shape in which it appears. And another effect upon me, since it affects me in a particular way.

Spirit. Earlier you looked for a bearer of the properties other than the space in which they are, something which endures through change other than space.

I. Yes, and this enduring something has been found. It is the force itself. It eternally remains the same in all change, and it is this force that assumes and bears properties.

Spirit. Let's take a look now at everything we've found so far. You feel yourself to be in a certain condition which you call red, smooth, sweet, etc. You know no more about that other than just that you feel this. Or do you know more? Is there something other in mere feeling than mere feeling?

I. No.

Spirit. Further, the determination of yourself as intelligence is that space which arises before you. Or do you know more about that?

I. Not at all.

Spirit. Between that felt condition and this space arising before you there is not the slightest connection other than that both happen to occur in your consciousness. Or do you see another connection?

I. I see none.

Spirit. But you also think. This simply is so. Just as it simply is so that you feel and intuit. And you know no more about it than that you just do it. You not only feel your condition, you also think it. But it gives you no complete thought. You are compelled to add something to your thought, a cause of it outside of you, an alien force. Do you know any more about this than that you happen to think this way, that you are compelled to think this way?

I. I can't know any more about it. I cannot think anything outside my thought, since by thinking it it becomes my thought and falls under the inevitable laws of my thought.

Spirit. Through this thinking there now arises for you a connection between your condition, which you feel, and space, which you intuit. Into this space you think the cause of your condition. Or is it not so?

I. It is so. That I produce the connection between the two in my consciousness only through my thinking, and that this connection is neither *felt* nor *intuited,* you have clearly proved. Of a connection *outside my consciousness,* however, I cannot speak. I have no way of conceiving such a connection. For, just in that I speak of it I know of it and, since this consciousness can only be a thinking, I think this connection. And it is quite the same connection which occurs in my ordinary natural consciousness, and no other. I have not gone beyond this consciousness by a hair's breadth, just as little as I can jump over myself. All attempts to think of such a connection in itself, of a thing in itself which is connected with the ego in itself, only ignore our own thinking. A remarkable forgetting that we can have no thought without thinking it. That thing in itself is a thought, one which is meant to be a fine thought which, however, no one wants to admit to having thought.

Spirit. From *you* then I need fear no objection against this proposition being definitely established, *that the consciousness of a thing outside of us is absolutely nothing more than the product of our own presentative capacity,* and that we know nothing more about the thing than, well, than we know about it, than we posit through our consciousness, that is, than we produce just by having consciousness, a consciousness determined in this way and subject to such laws?

I. I cannot object to that. It is so.

Spirit. No objection against the more daring expression of the same proposition: that in what we call knowledge and observation of things we always and ever only know and observe ourselves, and that in all our consciousness we simply know of nothing other than ourselves and our own determinations?

I say: to that you cannot have any objection either for, once *the whole realm of what is outside of us* only comes to be for us through our own consciousness, then there is no doubt that *the particular and manifold* of this external world does not come to be in any other way either. And if the connection of this external world *with us ourselves* is only a connection in our thoughts, then the connection *of the manifold things with each other is doubtless no other.* I could show you the laws according to which a multiplicity of objects come to be for you, objects which nevertheless are related to each other and reciprocally determine each other with iron necessity and in this way form a world system such as you have very well described to yourself; I could demonstrate these laws in your own thinking quite as clearly as I have just demonstrated there the genesis of an object as such and of its relation to you. And I refrain from this undertaking only because I find you must grant me the conclusion, which alone I care about, without such a demonstration.

I. I see it all and must grant you everything.

Spirit. And with this insight, mortal, be free and forever released from the fear which depressed and tortured you. You will now no longer tremble before a necessity which is only in your thought, no longer fear being oppressed by things which are your own products, no longer place yourself, the thinker, into the same class as objects of thought issuing from you yourself. As long as you could believe that a system of things such as you described to yourself really existed outside and independent of you, and that you yourself might be a link in the chain of this system, this fear was justified. Now, after you have seen that all this is only in and through yourself, you will without doubt not be afraid of what you have recognized as your own creature.

From this fear only I wanted to liberate you. Now you are redeemed from it and I leave you to yourself.

I. Stop, deceptive Spirit. Is this all the wisdom for which you gave me hope, and do you boast that you liberate me in this way? True, you liberate me: you absolve me of all dependence by transforming me and everything around me on which I might be dependent into nothing. You do away with necessity by doing away with and annihilating all being.

Spirit. Do you really think the danger is as great as that?

I. You can still mock? After your system?

Spirit. My system? Whatever we agreed to we produced in common. We both worked on it and your insight into everything was as good as my own. At present, however, it would be difficult for you to guess my true and complete thought.

I. Call your thoughts what you like. According to the above there is, in short, nothing, absolutely nothing but presentations, determinations of a consciousness as mere consciousness. But I consider a presentation to be a mere image, only a shadow of a reality. It cannot in itself satisfy me and is in itself not of the slightest value. I might allow the world of bodies outside of me to disappear into mere presentations and dissolve into shadows. It is of no great concern to me. But according to the above I myself disappear no less than it, I become a mere presenting without sense and without purpose. Or tell me yourself, is it otherwise?

Spirit. I say nothing at all in my name. Inquire yourself, help yourself.

I. I appear to myself as a body in space equipped with the means for sensing and acting, as a physical force determinable by a will. Of all this you will say what earlier you said generally about objects outside of me, the thinker, that it is a product of the combination of sensation, intuition, and thinking.

Spirit. Without doubt I will. If you request it I will even demonstrate step by step the laws according to which you appear in your consciousness as an organic body with such senses as a physical force, etc., and you will have to admit that I am right in everything I say.

I. I foresee it. As I had to admit that sweet, red, hard, and the like are nothing but my own inner condition, and that only through intuition and thought do they come to be regarded as transferred from me into space and as properties of a thing existing independently of me; just so I will have to admit that this body and its organic equipment is nothing but a sensualization into a determinate space-occupation of myself, the inwardly thinking being. I will have to admit that I, the mental being, the pure intelligence, and I, this body in the physical world, are one and the same thing, only seen from two sides, only apprehended in two different ways, the first by pure thinking, the second by external intuition.

Spirit. Were we to investigate the question, that would indeed be the result.

I. And this thinking mental being, that intelligence, which is transformed into an earthly body by intuition, what can it itself be according to these principles other than a product of my thinking, something purely and entirely thought up because it just happens that I have to invent in this way according to a law which is without origin or purpose and incomprehensible to me.

Spirit. Quite possibly.

I. You are becoming reticent and monosyllabic. It is not only possible; but according to these principles it is necessary. That perceiving, thinking, willing, intelligent being (or whatever you'd like to call it), which has the capacity to perceive, to think, etc., in which there is this capacity, or however you'd like to formulate this idea—how then do I arrive at it? Am I immediately conscious of it? How could I be? I am immediately conscious only of *actual determinate* perceiving, thinking, willing, as a particular event in me, not however of the capacity for these and still less of a being in which there is to be this capacity. I immediately intuit *this* particular thinking in which I am engaged at present and of *this* and *this* at other moments. And that is the extent of this inner intellectual intuition, this immediate consciousness. This inwardly intuited thinking itself I now think in turn, but according to the laws to which my thinking happens to be subject it is half a thing, something incomplete, for my thinking; just as above, the thinking of my mere condition in sensation was only half a thought. As above I added in thought an activity to the passivity without noticing it, so here to the *determined* (my actual thinking or willing) I add in thought a *determinable* (an infinitely manifold possible thinking or willing). I *must* do this, and for the same reason, without becoming aware of my adding as an operation of thought. This possible thinking I further conceive as a determinate whole; again because I must, since I cannot apprehend anything indeterminate, and thus it becomes for me a *finite capacity* for thought; and even, since in this thinking something existing independent of this thinking is presented to me, *a being, an entity,* which has this capacity.

Yet: from higher principles a still more vivid account can be given of how this thinking being produces itself merely through its own thinking. My thinking as such is genetic: it presupposes a *production* of what is *immediately given* and it describes this production. Intuition delivers the bare fact, and nothing more. Thought explains this fact and connects it with something else which in no way is given in intuition but is purely produced by thought itself, *from which it* (this fact) *proceeds.* So here. I am aware of a particular thought; so far and no further does intuitive consciousness get me. I think this determinate thought; that is, I let it come forth from an indeterminateness which, however, is determinable. This is how I proceed with everything determinate which occurs in immediate consciousness and from that comes all that series of capacities, and beings possessing these capacities, which I assume.

Spirit. You are therefore, even in respect of yourself, conscious only that you feel this or that determinate condition, that you intuit or think it in such a determinate way?

I. That *I* feel, *I* intuit, *I* think? That *I,* as the fundamental reality, bring forth sensation, intuition, and thought? Not at all. Your first principles don't even leave me that much.

Spirit. That too is possible.

I. That too is necessary. Just look for yourself: All that I know is my consciousness itself. All consciousness is either immediate or mediated. The first is self-consciousness, the second consciousness of what is not myself. What I call "I" is therefore nothing else whatever but a certain modification of consciousness, which modification is called "I" just because it is an immediate consciousness which returns into itself and is not directed outside. Since all consciousness is possible only on condition that there be immediate consciousness, it is evident that a consciousness of "I" accompanies all my presentations, is necessarily present in them even if it is not always explicitly noticed by me, and that at each moment of my consciousness I say: "I, I, I, and always I"—that is "I," and *not the particular thing outside of me of which I think at this moment.* In this way the "I" would disappear for me at each moment and again be renewed. For each new presentation a new "I" would come to be. And "I" would never mean anything other than "*non-thing.*"

This scattered self-consciousness is now brought together by thought, by mere thought, I say, and presented in the unity of an invented capacity. All presentations which are accompanied by the immediate consciousness of my presenting are, according to this invention, supposed to come from one and the same capacity which resides in one and the same being. And this is how I first come by the thought of the identity and personality of my "I" and of an active and real power of this person; necessarily a pure invention, since that capacity and that being itself are merely invented.

Spirit. You reason correctly.

I. And you take pleasure in that? I might therefore well say; *there is thinking.* Yet I can hardly even say that. So, more carefully, *thought appears:* the thought *that* I feel, intuit, think; but not the thought "*I feel, intuit, think.*" Only the first is fact, the second is added by invention.

Spirit. Well expressed!

I. Nowhere is there anything which endures, neither outside of me nor in me, but only ceaseless change. Nowhere do I know of any being, not even of my own. There is no being. *I myself* do not know at all and don't exist. There are *images:* they are all that exists and they know about themselves in the manner of images—images which drift by, without there being anything by which they drift; images which hang together through images; images which do not represent anything, without meaning and purpose. I myself am one

of these images. No, I am not even that, but only a distorted image
of these images. All reality is transformed into a fabulous dream,
without there being any life the dream is about, without there
being a mind which dreams; a dream which hangs together in a
dream of itself. *Intuition* is the dream; *thought* (the source of all
being and all reality which I imagine, of *my* being, my power, my
purposes), thought is the dream of this dream.

Spirit. You have understood everything very well. Do by all means
use the most cutting expressions and turns of phrase to make this
result hateful, as long as you must submit to it. And you must. You
have clearly seen that it just isn't otherwise. Or would you like to
take back your admission and justify this retraction with reasons?

I. Not at all. I have seen, and see clearly, that it is so. But I just
cannot *believe* it.

Spirit. You see it, but you just cannot believe it? That is something
else.

I. You are a malicious spirit. Your knowledge itself is malice, and
derives from malice, and I cannot be grateful that you have
brought me along this road.

Spirit. Shortsighted fellow! People like you call it wickedness if
one dares to see what there is, and if one sees as far as they do and
further. I have allowed you at your pleasure to infer the results of
our investigation, to discuss them, and to formulate them in hateful
expressions. Did you think that I was less familiar with these results
than you and that I did not understand just as well how with those
principles all reality would be thoroughly annihilated and transformed into a dream? Did you take me to be a blind worshipper
and panegyrist of this system as a complete system of the human
spirit?

You wanted to know, and got on quite the wrong road for that.
You looked for knowledge where no knowledge can reach, and had
already persuaded yourself that you understand something which
is contrary to the inner nature of all understanding. I found you in
that condition. I wanted to free you from your false knowledge, not
to teach you the truth.

You wanted to know about your knowledge. Are you surprised
that on this road too you learned about nothing more than your
knowledge, which is what you wanted; and would you have it some
other way? What comes to be in and through knowledge is only

knowledge. But all knowledge is only a depicting, and in it something is always demanded which would correspond to the image. This demand can be satisfied by no knowledge, and a system of knowledge is necessarily a system of mere images, without any reality, meaning, and purpose. Did you expect something else? Do you want to change the inner nature of your mind and expect your knowledge to be more than knowledge?

The reality which you thought you had already caught sight of, a sensible world existing independently of you whose slave you feared to become, has disappeared for you. This whole sensible world comes to be only through knowledge and is itself our knowledge. But knowledge is not reality just because it is knowledge. You have seen the deception and, without denying your better insight, can never give yourself over to it again. And this is the one merit which I claim for the system we have just found together: it destroys and annihilates error. It cannot give truth, for in itself it is absolutely empty. But you are looking for something real lying beyond the mere image. This is your right, as I well know. And you are looking for a reality other than the one which has just been annihilated. I know that as well. But your effort would be in vain were you to try to produce it through your knowledge and from your knowledge and to grasp it with your knowledge. If you have no other means of grasping it, then you will never find it.

But you have such a means. Put some life into it and warm it up, and you will attain to complete tranquility. I leave you alone with yourself.

BOOK THREE
Faith

Your discussion has crushed me, terrible Spirit. But you refer me to myself. And what would I be if anything outside of me could irretrievably crush me? I will, oh I will surely follow your advice.

What are you looking for, my lamenting heart? What is it that rouses your indignation against a system to which my intellect cannot make the slightest objection?

This: I want something which lies beyond mere mental presentations, which is there, was there, and will be there even if there were no presentation; something which the mind only looks at without producing it or making the least change in it. A mere presentation I regard as a deceptive image. My presentations are to refer to something, and if nothing outside of knowledge corresponds to any of my knowledge then I think I will have been defrauded of my whole life. 'Nothing exists anywhere outside my mind' is a thought which natural sense considers ridiculously stupid, a thought which no human being could assert with complete seriousness and which requires no refutation. For the educated judgment which knows the deep reasons for it, reasons irrefutable through mere ratiocination, it is a crushing and annihilating thought.

And what is it, then, that lies outside the mind which I embrace with such ardent yearning? What is the power with which it forces itself upon me? What is the central point in my soul to which it attaches itself, a point destructible only together with my soul itself?

Your vocation is not merely to know, but *to act* according to your knowledge. This is what I clearly hear in my inmost soul as soon as

I collect myself for a moment and pay attention to myself. You do not exist for idle self-observation or to brood over devout sensations. No, you exist for activity. Your activity, and your activity alone, determines your worth.

This voice leads me out of mental presentations, out of mere knowledge, to something which lies outside of it and is its complete opposite; to something which is more and higher than all knowledge and contains the final purpose of knowledge itself within it. When I act I will without doubt know that I act and how I act. This knowledge is not the acting itself but only looks at it. This voice then announces to me precisely what I was looking for, something lying outside of knowledge and in its being quite independent of it.

It is so, I know it immediately. But I have engaged in philosophical speculation. The doubts which this stirred up in me will secretly persist and disturb me. Having put myself into this position I can never be fully satisfied until everything I accept has been justified before the judgment seat of speculation. I must therefore ask myself: how does it become so? What is the origin of that voice in me which directs me beyond presentations?

There is in me a drive to absolute independent self-activity. I find nothing more intolerable than only to be in another, for another, and through another. I want to be and become something for and through myself. I feel this drive just as soon as ever I become aware of myself; it is indivisibly united with the consciousness of myself.

I make the feeling of this drive clear to myself in thought and, as it were, insert eyes into the intrinsically blind drive by means of concepts. In keeping with this drive I ought to act as an absolutely independent being. That is how I apprehend and translate that drive. *I* am to be independent. Who am I? Subject and object in one, the omnipresent knower and known, the intuiting and the intuited, the thinker and the thought at once. As both I am to be through myself what I am, to originate concepts simply through myself, and simply through myself to produce a condition lying beyond the concept. But how is the latter possible? To nothing I simply can connect no being. Nothing will never become something. My objective thinking is necessarily mediating. A being, however, which is *connected* to another being is ipso facto *caused* by this other being and is no first and original being, the inception of a series, but a derived being. *Connect* I must; but I cannot connect to *a being*.

My thinking and originating of a purpose, however, is in its nature absolutely free and brings forth something from nothing. I would have to connect my acting to such a thinking if I am to regard it as free and as simply proceeding from myself.

I conceive of my independence as "I" in the following manner, therefore. I ascribe to myself the capacity to originate a concept simply because I originate it, to originate *this* concept because I originate it in the absolute sovereignty of myself as intelligence. I further ascribe to myself the capacity to exhibit this concept through a real act outside the concept. That is, I ascribe to myself a real effective power of bringing forth being, which is something quite different from the mere capacity of concepts. Those concepts, called purposes, are not, like concepts of knowledge, the *after*-copy of a given, but rather the *prior* designs for something yet to be produced. The real power must lie outside of them and exist as such for itself. It should only receive its determination from them, and knowledge should only look on. In consequence of this drive I really suppose myself to have such an independence.

Here, it seems, is the point to which the consciousness of all reality is connected. The real efficacy of my concept and the real power to act which in consequence of that efficacy I must ascribe to myself is that point. In the meantime let things be as they may with the reality of a sensible world outside of me. I have reality and I apprehend it. It lies in me and is native to myself.

I think this real power of mine to act, but I do not *think it up*. The immediate feeling of my drive to independent activity is behind this thought. Thought does nothing more than to represent this feeling and to take it up into its own form, the form of thought. This procedure seems able to hold up before the judgment seat of speculation.

What? Will I again knowingly and intentionally deceive myself? This procedure can by no means hold up before that strict tribunal.

I feel in myself an urge and a striving outward. This seems to be true, and to be the only thing that is true in this matter. This urge, of course, appears to me as having its origin in me and as being directed at an activity which also has its origin in me, since I am the one who feels this urge, and since I cannot go beyond myself either with my whole consciousness nor in particular with my feeling; and

I cannot so go beyond myself, since this consciousness and feeling, i.e., since I myself am the last point where I apprehend this urge. But could it not, nevertheless, be the urging of an outside force, invisible to me and unnoticed by me, and could not that opinion of independence be merely a deception due to my field of vision being restricted to myself? I have no reason to assume that this is so, but just as little do I have reason to deny it. I must admit that I simply know nothing about it, nor can I know.

Do I then even feel that real power of action which, marvelously enough, I ascribe to myself without knowing anything about it? By no means; it is the *determinable* invented according to the well-known law of thought by which all capacities and forces come to be, appended to the *determined,* the likewise invented real action.

Is this being directed beyond the bare concept to its supposed realization anything other than the usual and well-known procedure of all objective thinking, since it does not want to be mere thought but also to refer to something outside of thought. By what sophistry is this procedure to be more valid here than elsewhere? Is it to be more significant if to the thought of an act of thinking is added a reality of this thinking, than if to the thought of this table a real table were added? What reasons could I adduce against the following explanation: 'the concept of a purpose, a particular determination of events in me, appears in two ways, partly as something subjective, a thought, and partly as something objective, an act?' This explanation would doubtless not lack a genetic derivation either.

I do, however, feel this urge, I say. But surely I say this myself, and think it as I say it? Do I really feel, or do I only think that I feel? Is not everything I call feeling only something set before me by my objectifying thought, and perhaps properly the first point of transition of all objectification? And do I really think, or do I only think that I'm thinking? And do I think that I am really thinking, or do I only think a thought of thought? What can prevent speculation from asking such questions and from continuing to ask them indefinitely? What can I answer and where is there a point at which I could call a halt to its questions? I know, of course, and must concede this to speculation, that one can reflect on every determination of consciousness and produce a new consciousness of the first consciousness, that in doing this one always moves immediate consciousness one step higher and obscures and makes doubtful the first, and that this ladder has no highest rung. I know that all skepticism is based on this procedure, and I know that the system[1] which dismayed me so deeply is based on the pursuit and explicit awareness of this procedure.

I know that if with this system I don't want only to play another confusing game, but really want to live by it, I will have to refuse obedience to that inner voice. I cannot want to act, for according to that system I cannot know whether I can act. I can never believe that I am really acting. What appears to me as my act I must consider to be quite meaningless and a mere deceptive image. My life will then be purged of all seriousness and interest, and it will be transformed, just like my thought, into a mere game which comes from nowhere and goes nowhere.

Shall I refuse obedience to that inner voice? I will not. I will freely give myself the determination which that drive indicates in me, and in this resolution I will at the same time seize the thought of its reality and truthfulness and of the reality of everything it presupposes. I will remain with the standpoint of natural thought to which this drive brings me and reject all those ruminations and sophistical subtleties which could only make its truthfulness doubtful.

Now I understand you, sublime Spirit. I have found the means by which to take hold of this reality and with it probably at the same time all the rest of reality. Knowledge is not this means. No knowledge can be its own foundation and proof. Every knowledge presupposes something still higher as its foundation, and this ascent has no end. It is faith, this voluntary acquiescence in the view which naturally presents itself to us because only on this view can we fulfill our vocation; it is that which first gives approval to knowledge and raises to certainty and conviction what without it could be mere deception. Faith is no knowledge, but a decision of the will to recognize the validity of knowledge.

I will then forever hold fast to this expression, which is no mere verbal distinction but a true, deeply founded distinction of the most important consequence for my whole disposition. All my conviction

---

1. [The "system" of Book Two is meant.]

is only faith; and it proceeds from my disposition, not from the intellect. Now that I know this I will not take part in disputation, for I see in advance that nothing can be gained by it. I will not allow myself to be confused by it because the source of my conviction is higher than all disputation. It wouldn't occur to me to want to foist this conviction onto another person with arguments, and I won't be surprised if such an undertaking fails. I have adopted my way of thinking initially for myself, not for others, and only want to justify it for myself. Whoever shares my disposition, a sincere good will, will also come to hold my conviction: without this good will, however, there is no way of producing it. Once I know this I also know the point of departure for all education of myself as well as others: it is the will, not the intellect. If only the former is steadily and sincerely directed at the good, the latter will of itself apprehend the true. If only the latter is exercised while the former is neglected, then nothing more will come of it than a facility for racking one's brain with intellectual quibbling, which leads to nothing. Once I know this I can beat down all false knowledge which might rise up against my faith. I know that every supposed truth, which is to be produced by mere thinking without having its roots in faith, will surely be false and fallacious, since bare and pure cognition carried out with logical thoroughness only leads to the insight that we can know nothing. I know that such false knowledge will never find anything other than what by faith it has first put into its premises, from which it perhaps draws further incorrect inferences. Once I know this I possess the touchstone of all truth and all conviction. Truth has its origin in conscience alone. Whatever is opposed to conscience and to the possibility and resolution of acting according to conscience, is surely false and it is not possible to be convinced of it, even if I cannot discover the fallacies that produced it.

It is no different with any human being who has ever seen the light of day. Without even being aware of it they apprehend all reality which is there for them only by faith; and this faith imposes itself upon them together with their existence, innate in them all. And how could it be otherwise? If in mere knowledge, in mere looking at and thinking about, there is simply no reason for taking our presentations to be more than mere images, though imposed on us with necessity, why do we all take them to be more and provide them with something existing independent of all presentation as their cause? If we all have the ability and the urge to go beyond our first natural view, then why do so few go beyond it and even defend themselves with a kind of exasperation if one tries to get them to do so? What is it that holds them captive in that first natural view? It is not reasons, for there are none that can do it. Rather it is their *interest* in a reality they want to produce—the good person, simply to produce it; the common, sensual person, to enjoy it. No one who is alive can part with this interest nor with the faith which this interest brings with it. We are all born in faith. Whoever is blind in this regard will blindly follow its secret and irresistible promptings. Whoever can see will follow with open eyes, and will believe because he wants to believe.

What unity and completion in itself, what dignity of human nature! Our thinking is not founded on itself, independent of our drives and inclinations; a human being does not consist of two parts running parallel to each other, but is absolutely a unit. All our thinking is founded in our drives, and as an individual's inclinations are, so is his knowledge. These drives impose a certain way of thinking upon us only as long as we don't see the compulsion. But compulsion disappears as soon as it is seen, and now it is no longer the drives which shape our way of thinking through themselves, but it is we ourselves who, in keeping with our drives, shape our own way of thinking.

But I am to open my eyes; I am to come to know myself thoroughly; I am to see that compulsion; that is my vocation. I am, therefore, to shape my own way of thinking for myself and, under that presupposition, will do so necessarily. I will then be absolutely independent, having completed and prepared myself. The wellspring of all the rest of my thinking and of my life, that from which flows all that can be in me and for me and through me, the innermost spirit of my spirit is not an alien spirit but is simply produced by myself in the truest sense of the word. I am thoroughly my own creation. I could have blindly followed the promptings of my own spiritual nature. I did not want to be nature, but my own work; and I have become so by willing it. I could have made the natural view of my mind doubtful and obscure with endless quibbling. I have adopted it freely because I wanted to adopt it. The way of thinking which I have carefully, intentionally, and with consideration chosen from among other possible ways of thinking, because I recognized it to be the only one appropriate to my dignity and vocation. Freely and consciously I have returned to the standpoint where my nature had left me. I accept what my nature also says. But I do not accept it because I must. Rather, I believe it because I want to.

I am filled with reverence for the lofty purposes of my intellect. It is no longer that playful and empty image-maker of nothing and for nothing; it has been given to me for a great purpose. I am entrusted with cultivating it for this purpose. This task I have in hand and I will be held accountable for it. I have it in hand. I know immediately (and I believe this testimony of my consciousness without further quibbling) that I do not have to let my thoughts flutter about blindly and to no purpose, but that I am able at will to rouse and to direct my attention, to turn it away from one object and fix it on another. I know that it is only up to me not to stop the investigation of this object until I have fully penetrated it and until the most complete conviction is made evident by it. I know that it is neither blind necessity which imposes a certain system of thinking upon me, nor empty chance which plays with my thoughts, but it is I who am thinking, and that I can think about what I want to think about. Through thoughtful consideration I have just now found even more. I have found that only I myself produce through myself my whole way of thinking and the particular view I have of truth in general, while it is up to me whether I rob myself of all sense of truth by philosophical rumination or devote myself to it with faithful obedience. My whole way of thinking and the cultivation of my intellect, as well as the objects to which I direct it, depend entirely on me. Correct insight is merit; perversion of my capacity for knowledge is thoughtlessness; obfuscation, error, and unbelief are guilt.

There is only one point to which I have ceaselessly to direct all my thought: what I ought to do and how I can best carry out what I am bidden. All my thoughts must relate to my activity. It must be possible to see it as a means to this purpose, even if only remotely so. Apart from that it is an empty pointless game, a waste of time and energy, and a perversion of a noble capacity which I was given with a quite different intention.

I may hope, I may surely promise myself to carry on such thinking successfully. The natural world in which I have to act is not an alien being brought about without consideration for me, a being into which I could never penetrate. It is formed by my own laws of thought and must surely agree with them. It must surely be everywhere transparent and knowable and accessible through and through. Everywhere it expresses nothing other than my own relations to myself, so surely as I can hope to know myself, as surely may I promise myself to come to know it. As long as I seek what it is my business to seek, I will find. As long as I ask what it is my business to ask, I will receive an answer.

I

That inner voice in which I believe, and for the sake of which I believe everything else which I believe, does not bid me simply to act. This is impossible. All these general propositions are only formed through my voluntarily paying attention to and reflecting on several facts, but themselves never express a fact. It, this voice of my conscience, tells me, in each particular situation in my life, what I definitely have to do or avoid in this situation. It accompanies me, if only I listen to it attentively, through all the events of my life, and it never denies me its advice[2] when I have to act. It immediately justifies conviction and irresistibly elicits my assent; it is not possible for me to quarrel with it.

To listen to it, to obey it sincerely and unhesitatingly without fear and quibbling, this is my only vocation, the whole purpose of my existence. My life ceases to be an empty game without truth and meaning. Something ought to happen simply because it ought to happen: that which my conscience requires of me, just of me who finds himself in this situation. That it may happen, for that, for that alone I exist. I have understanding so that I may recognize it, and strength so that I may accomplish it.

2. [Reading *Belohnung* as *Belehrung*.]

Only through these commandments of conscience do truth and reality come into my presentations. I cannot refuse them my attention and my obedience without giving up my vocation.

Nor can I refuse to believe in the reality which they bring along without likewise denying my vocation. It is simply true, without further testing and justification, it is the first truth and the ground of all other truth and certainty, that I ought to obey that voice. In this way of thinking, therefore, everything becomes true and certain for me which is presupposed as true and certain by the possibility of such an obedience.

I am aware of appearances in space to which I transfer the concept of myself; I think of them as beings like myself. Speculative philosophy, taken to its conclusion, has taught me or will teach me that these supposed rational beings outside of me are nothing but products of my own mind, that I just happen to be compelled, according to demonstrable laws of my thought, to present the concept of myself outside of myself and that, by the same laws, this concept can only be transferred to certain determinate intuitions. But the voice of my conscience calls to me: whatever these beings may be in and for themselves, you ought to treat them as self-subsistent, free, autonomous beings completely independent of you. Presuppose as already known that they can determine their purposes quite on their own and independently of you. Never interfere with the pursuit of these purposes, but rather promote them as much as you can. Respect their freedom. With love take up their purposes like your own. This is how I ought to act. All my thinking ought to be directed to such action; and my thinking will and must necessarily be so directed to acting that way if only I have resolved to obey the voice of my conscience. I will therefore always regard those beings as beings which exist for themselves and are there independently of me, as beings which set themselves purposes and carry them out. From this standpoint I will not be able to see them any other way, and that speculation will disappear before my eyes like an empty dream.

I just said that I *think* of them as beings like myself. But strictly speaking it is not thought by which they are first presented to me as such. It is the voice of conscience, the commandment, "here limit your freedom, here suppose and respect other purposes," which is first translated into the thought, "here is certainly and truly a self-existent being like myself." To see them otherwise I must first deny the voice of my conscience in life and disregard it in speculation.

I am presented with other appearances which I do not take to be beings like myself but rather things devoid of reason. Speculation has no difficulty demonstrating how the presentation of such things is developed solely from my presenting capacity and its necessary modes of activity. But I also grasp those things through need, desire, and enjoyment. Something comes to be food and drink for me not through concepts but through hunger, thirst, and satisfaction. I am surely coerced to believe in the reality of anything which threatens my sensible existence or which alone can preserve it. Conscience enters here in that it hallows and at the same time limits this natural drive. You ought to preserve, exercise, and strengthen yourself and your physical strength, for this strength is counted upon in the plan of reason. But you can only preserve it by using it purposefully, by using it in a way commensurate with the inner laws proper to these things. And apart from you there are still many others like you whose strength is counted upon like yours, and which can only be preserved in the same way as yours. Grant them the same use for their part as is required of you for yours. Honor their due as their property; treat what belongs to you purposefully as yours. That is how I ought to act, and my thinking must be commensurate with this acting. I am therefore compelled to regard these things as subject to their own natural laws, which are independent of me even though they are to be known by me; and thus to ascribe to them, at any rate, an existence independent of me. I am compelled to believe in such laws; it becomes my task to investigate them, and that empty speculation disappears like fog before the heat of the sun.

In short, bare pure being that does not concern me and that I would intuit just for the sake of intuition does not exist for me at all; only through its relation to me does anything whatever exist for me. But everywhere only one relation to me is possible, and all others are only subspecies of this one: my vocation to act ethically. My world is the object and sphere of my duties and absolutely nothing else. Another world, or other properties of my world, do not exist for me. My whole capacity and any finite capacity is insufficient for apprehending another world. Everything that exists for me imposes its existence and reality on me only through this relation, and only through this relation do I apprehend it. And for any other existence I have no organ at all.

To the question, whether indeed there is a world such as I experience, I can answer nothing fundamental and beyond all doubt except this: I certainly and truly have these determinate duties that
present themselves to me as duties *against* such and *in* such objects,
these particular duties which I cannot conceive nor carry out other
than in a world such as I experience. The world of the senses and
belief in the reality of that world is produced in no other way than
through the conception of a moral world, even for the person who
may never have thought about his own moral vocation (if there
could be such a person), or, if he should have thought about it, has
not the least intention of fulfilling it at any time in the indefinite
future. Even if he does not apprehend this world through the
thought of his *duties,* he will yet surely do so through the demand of
his *rights.* What, perhaps, he never expects of himself he will,
however, surely expect of others in relation to himself: that they
treat him with consideration, thoughtfully, and purposefully, not as
a nonrational thing but as a free and independent being. And so, if
they are even to be able to meet this requirement, he will be obliged
to think of them too as considerate, free, self-sufficient, and independent of the mere power of nature. Even if, say, in the use and
enjoyment of objects around him he never has any purpose other
than to enjoy them, he at least demands this enjoyment as a right
with which others must not interfere. And thus he apprehends
even the nonrational world of the senses by means of a moral
conception. These claims to respect for his rationality and independence and preservation no one who is alive and conscious can give
up. Seriousness and denial of doubt and belief in a reality at least
are connected in his soul with these claims, if they are not connected with the recognition of an inner moral law. Just take a
person who, for some reason other than merely to see what speculation is capable of, denies his own moral vocation and your existence and the existence of a physical world, and lay rough hands on
him; just introduce his principles into life and behave as though
either he does not exist at all or is just a piece of raw matter; he will
soon have done with joking and become seriously annoyed with
you. He will seriously rebuke you for treating him so. He will assert
that you should not treat him so, that he will not permit it. He will
therefore admit to you by acts that you can after all act on him, that
he exists and that *you* exist and that there exists *a medium through*

which you can act on him, and that *you* at least have duties toward him.

It is not, therefore, the influence of supposed things outside of us, which after all exist for us and we for them only so far as we already know of them; and just as little is it an empty imaging through our imagination and thought, the products of which would after all really appear as such products, as empty images; it is not these but the necessary belief in our freedom and strength, in the reality of our acting, and in specific laws of human acting that justifies all consciousness of a reality existing outside of us, a consciousness which itself is only a faith since it is based on faith, but a faith which necessarily follows from consciousness. We are compelled to accept that we act at all and that we ought to act in a certain way. We are compelled to accept a certain sphere for this acting. This sphere is the real world, which indeed exists as we encounter it. And conversely, this world is absolutely nothing other than that sphere and in no way extends beyond it. Consciousness of the real world proceeds from that need to act; the need to act does not proceed from the consciousness of the world. The need to act is first, not consciousness of the world, which is derived. We do not act because we know, but we know because we are meant to act; practical reason is the root of all reason. The laws of action for rational beings are *immediately* certain: their world is certain only by virtue of the fact *that those laws are certain.* We cannot renounce those laws without having the world and, with it, ourselves sink into absolute nothingness. We raise ourselves out of this nothingness and maintain ourselves above this nothingness only through our morality.

II

There is something which I absolutely ought to do, so that it occur; and something which I ought to refrain from doing, so that it not occur. But can I act without having in view a purpose outside the act, without directing my intention to something that first can and ought to become possible through my act and through it alone? Can I will without willing something? Never! This would wholly contradict the nature of my mind. In my thinking each of my *acts* is

connected immediately and according to the laws of thought themselves to a *being* which lies in the future, a situation to which the
activity relates as cause to effect. But this purpose of my activity
should not be set for me in itself, as a natural need for example,
and have the mode of action determined only afterwards according
to this purpose. I should not have a purpose just because I happen
to have it, and only afterwards consider how I must act to fulfill this
purpose; my act should not depend on the purpose. Rather, I am
simply to act in a certain way just because I ought; that is the first.
My inner voice tells me that something results from this mode of
activity. This something now necessarily becomes a purpose for me
because I ought to carry out the act which is the means to this
purpose and only to it. I will that something be realized because I
ought to act so as to realize it. I am not hungry because there is
food available to me, but rather something becomes food for me
because I am hungry. Just so, I do not act as I act because something is my purpose, but rather something becomes my purpose
because I ought so to act. I do not have the point to which I want to
draw my line already in view in advance, and now let its position
determine the direction and the angle my line is to take; rather, I
simply draw my line at a right angle, and by that the points which
my line must meet are determined. The purpose does not determine the content of the commandment; on the contrary, the immediately given content of the commandment determines the
purpose.

I say that it is the commandment of action itself which through
itself gives me a purpose. Whatever it is in me that compels me to
think that I ought so to act compels me to believe that something
will result from this act. It opens the prospect of another world to
my mind's eye, a world which really is a *world,* a *situation,* and not an
action, but a *different and better* world than the one that exists for my
sense of sight. It makes me desire this better world, to embrace and
long for it with my whole being, to live only in it and be satisfied
only with it. That commandment is itself my guarantee for the sure
attainment of this purpose. The same disposition with which I direct and attach my whole thought and life to this commandment
and see nothing apart from it, also brings with it the unshakable
conviction that its promise is true and certain, and eliminates the
possibility of even thinking the reverse. As I live in obedience, I at

the same time live in the intuition of its purpose, live in the better world which it promises me.

Even a mere look at the world as it is apart from the commandment already arouses the inner wish, the longing—no, not a mere longing—the absolute demand for a better world. I take a look at the present relation of people to each other and to nature, at the weakness of their powers, and the strength of their desires and passions. Irresistibly it resounds in my inner being: it is impossible that things should remain as they are, everything must, oh it must, become different and better.

I simply cannot think of the present situation of mankind as the final and permanent one, simply cannot think of it as mankind's whole and final destiny. If it were, then everything would be dream and deception; and it would not be worth the trouble of having lived, of having played this ever-recurring game that goes nowhere and means nothing. Only so far as I may see this condition as a means to something better, as a point of transition to something higher and more perfect, does it come to have value for me. I can bear it, respect it, and gladly do my part in it, not for the sake of this condition itself, but for the sake of the better thing which it prepares. I do not feel at home in the present nor feel at ease there for a moment. Irresistibly I am repelled by it. My whole life incessantly flows toward the future and better state of things.

Am I to eat and drink only to get hungry and thirsty and eat and drink again, until the grave opened at my feet devours me and I myself have sprouted from the ground as food? Have I fathered beings like myself so that they too might eat and drink and die and leave behind beings like them who will do the same as I have already done? What is the purpose of this circle ever returning into itself, of this game ever beginning anew in the same way, a game in which everything comes to be only to pass away, and passes away only to become again as it already was? Why this monster that ceaselessly devours itself so that it can give birth to itself again, and gives birth to itself so that it can devour itself again?

Never can this be the destiny of my being and of all being. There must be something that *exists* because it has come to be, and then *abides,* and can never come to be again once it has come to be. This abiding being must produce itself in the changing world of transitory things, must endure in it and be carried along unharmed on the flood of time.

Mankind still toils to wrest its sustenance and survival from recalcitrant nature. The majority of people are still bent under hard labor all their lives to produce nourishment for themselves and for the minority that thinks for them. Immortal spirits must still direct all their thought and ingenuity and all their effort to the soil that bears their nourishment. It still happens frequently, when a working man has done his work and, thanks to it, looks forward to his own survival and to that of his work, that bad weather destroys in a moment what he had built up slowly and carefully over the years, and that this industrious and prudent man is abandoned to hunger and misery through no fault of his own. It still happens frequently enough that floods, storms, and volcanoes desolate whole countries and mix works which carry the imprint of a rational mind into the wild chaos of death and destruction together with the master craftsmen who built them. Diseases still sweep people into an untimely grave, men in the flower of their strength, and children whose existence ends without fruit or consequence. Plagues still move through flourishing states and leave the few who escape them orphaned and lonely, robbed of the accustomed support of their fellows, and do everything in their power to return to wilderness the land which the industry of people had already made their property. That is how it is: it cannot be true that it ought always to remain so. No work that bears the imprint of reason and was undertaken to expand the power of reason can be completely lost in the course of the ages. The sacrifices which the unruly violence of nature extorts from reason must at least exhaust, satiate, and appease that violence. The force that has caused harm beyond measure can no longer be allowed to do so; it cannot be destined to renew itself, but must from now on be used up forever in one outbreak. All those outbreaks of raw violence before which human strength dwindles to nothing, those devastating hurricanes, those earthquakes, those volcanoes, can be nothing other than the last resistance of the wild mass against the lawful, life-giving, purposeful march of progress to which it is compelled contrary to its own impulses; nothing other than the last convulsive strokes in the formation of our planet, which is now reaching completion. The resistance must gradually become weaker and finally be exhausted since there can be nothing in this lawful advance that might renew its strength. That formation must finally be completed and our destined home be finished. Nature must gradually enter a condition which allows one to calculate and reckon safely on its regular pace, and which keeps its force steady in a definite relation with the power which is destined to control it—the power of man. Insofar as this relation already exists and the purposeful formation of nature has already got a firm foothold, the works of man, simply because they exist and through effects beyond the intention of their builders, shall themselves again intervene in nature and constitute there a new animating principle. Cultivated lands shall animate and moderate the inert and hostile atmosphere of primeval forests, deserts, and swamps. Ordered and varied cultivation shall spread the impulse to new life and fertility all around, and the sun shall pour out its most animating rays into an atmosphere in which a healthy, industrious, and artistic people breathes. Science, first awakened by the pressure of need, shall later penetrate into the invariable laws of nature more thoughtfully and calmly, survey the whole power of this nature, and learn to calculate its possible developments. While remaining close to living and active nature and following in its footsteps, it shall conceive of a new nature. And each insight that reason has wrested from nature shall be preserved in the course of time and become the foundation for new knowledge in the collective understanding of our species. In this way, nature is to become ever more transparent to us until we can see into its most secret core, and human power, enlightened and armed by its discoveries, shall control it without effort and peacefully maintain any conquest once it is made. Gradually no greater expenditure of mechanical work shall be required than the human body needs for its development, cultivation, and health, and this work shall cease to be a burden; for a rational being is not meant to be a bearer of burdens.

But it is not nature, it is freedom itself that causes most of the disorders and the most terrible ones among humanity. Man's most cruel enemy is man. Lawless hordes of savages still stray through immense barren lands. They encounter each other in the desert and make a festive meal of each other. Or, where culture has finally united the wild rabble under law into a nation, nations attack each other with the power which unification and law gave them. Defying hardships and privation, armies march through the peaceful countryside. They catch sight of each other, and the sight of someone like themselves is the signal to murder. Equipped with the greatest inventions of the human mind, navies ply the oceans. Men press through storm and wave in search of other men on the lonely, inhospitable expanse. They find them and defy the rage of the elements so as to be able to destroy them with their own hands. In the interior of states themselves, where people appear to be unified in equality under the law, it is for the most part still cunning and power that rule under the venerable name of the law. Here war is conducted all the more shamefully because it does not declare itself to be war and even deprives the injured party of the privilege of defending himself against unjust power. Small cliques loudly rejoice over the ignorance, the folly, the depravity, and the misery in which the greater part of their fellows are sunk, and openly make it their chief purpose to keep them in that condition and to plunge them down more deeply, so as to keep them in slavery forever—and to ruin anyone who might venture to enlighten and improve them. It is still nowhere possible to propose any improvement without stirring up a host of the most varied self-seeking purposes and inciting them to war, without uniting the most diverse and incompatible attitudes in single-minded opposition to it. The good is always weaker, for it is simple and can only be loved for its own sake. Evil entices each individual with the promise which is the most tempting for him, and the perverted, though they constantly quarrel with each other, declare a truce as soon as the good comes into view and move against it with the combined strength of their perdition. However, there is hardly any need for their opposition, for the good themselves still fight each other owing to misunderstanding and error, to mistrust and secret self-love—they often fight all the harder the more seriously each seeks to realize what he, from his perspective, takes to be best. And so, in their fight with each other, they dissipate a strength which even combined would hardly tip the balance against evil. One blames the other for his impetuous impatience, for being too hasty and unable to wait until the success of the good has been properly prepared, while another accuses that one of being too timid and cowardly to do anything, of being prepared, against his better judgment, to leave everything as it is, so that the time for action will probably never come for him. And only the Omniscient could say whether one of them is right in this dispute and, if so, which one. Almost everyone takes the business which *he* sees to be most clearly necessary and for which he is most qualified, to be the most important and pressing, to be the point from which all other improvement must proceed. He calls upon all good people to unite their strength with his and to subordinate it to him for the execution of his purpose, and takes it to be a betrayal of the good work if they refuse. At the same time the others for their part make the same demands on him and accuse him of the same betrayal if he refuses. In this way all good intentions among people seem to disappear in vain endeavors and leave no trace of their existence behind. Meanwhile, everything goes on as well or badly as it can without these efforts, through the blind mechanism of nature, and will go on forever.

Will go on forever? Never—unless the whole of human existence is a purposeless and meaningless game. It cannot be that those savage tribes shall forever remain savage: no race can be born with all the capacities for perfect humanity and be destined never to develop these capacities and never to become more than something for which the nature of a clever animal would be wholly adequate. Those savages are meant to be the ancestors of strong, cultured, and dignified generations. Apart from that no purpose is conceivable for their existence, nor is the possibility of this existence in a rationally ordered world comprehensible. Savage tribes can be cultivated, for they already have been, and the most cultivated people of the New World are themselves descended from savages. Whether culture develops directly and naturally in human society, or whether it must always come by instruction and example from outside, and the first source of all human culture is to be sought in superhuman instruction—in the same way in which those who were savages in the past have now attained to culture, present-day savages will gradually receive it too. They will, however, pass through the same dangers and corruption of the first merely sensuous culture, which at present oppress educated peoples; but they will thereby, nevertheless, be unified with the great whole of humanity and become capable of taking part in its further progress.

Our species is destined to unify itself into one single body, thoroughly acquainted with itself in all its parts and everywhere educated in the same way. The nature and even the passions and vices of men have tended toward this goal from the beginning. We have already come a long way on the road to this goal, which is the condition of further common progress, and we may surely count on reaching it when the time is right. Don't ask history whether men have on the whole become more moral! They have developed an extensive, encompassing, powerful free will, but their situation has made it nearly necessary for them to use this free will almost only for evil. Nor ask whether, in its concentration on a few points, the aesthetic cultivation and intellectual culture of the ancient world may not have been superior to that of more recent time. It could be that we would receive a humiliating answer and that in this respect humanity might seem not to have advanced with age but retreated. But ask history at what time the existing culture had its greatest extent and when the greatest number of individuals had a share in it, and you will undoubtedly find that from the beginning of history down to the present day the few brilliant concentrations of culture have expanded outward from their centers, and taken hold of one individual after another and one nation after another, and that this further expansion of culture is continuing before our eyes. And this was the first goal of humanity on its endless path. Until this has been reached, until the existing culture of every age has spread over the whole populated globe and our species is capable of the most unrestricted communication with itself, one nation must await the other and one continent the other on the common path, and each must bring its centuries of apparent standstill or retreat as a sacrifice to the common bond for the sake of which alone they exist. Once this first goal has been reached, once everything useful which has been found at one end of the earth will immediately be communicated and known to all, then mankind will without interruption, without standstill and retreat, with common strength, and in a single stride elevate itself to a culture which is at present beyond our conception.

Within those remarkable associations brought together by mindless chance which we call states, after they have achieved stability even for a time, and the resistance aroused by recent subjugation has died away and the ferment of the various powers has settled, abuse receives a kind of established form through its continuity and general tolerance; and the ruling classes, in the uncontested enjoyment of the privileges they had won, have nothing more to do than to expand those privileges and to give their expansion the same established form as well. Driven by their insatiability they will expand them from generation to generation and never say, "This much is enough," until finally oppression will have reached its limit and become entirely unbearable, and despair will give the oppressed a strength which centuries of broken spirit had been unable to give them. They will then no longer tolerate anyone among them who is not satisfied with being and remaining everyone's equal. To guard against mutual violence among themselves and against new oppression they will all impose the same obligations on each other. Their agreements, in which everyone decides what he decides about himself, and not about a subordinate whose suffering will never hurt him and whose fate will never touch him; these agreements, whereby no one can hope that he will be the one to *practice* authorized injustice, but each must fear that he will be the one to *suffer* it; these agreements, which alone deserve to be called law-making, which is something quite different from those decrees of the allied masters to the countless herds of their slaves; these agreements will necessarily be just and found a true state in which each individual will, through concern for his own security, be irresistibly compelled to respect the security of all without exception since, in consequence of the arrangement made, every injury he seeks to inflict on another will not befall the other but inevitably fall back upon himself.

By the establishment of this one true state, this solid foundation of internal peace, the possibility of external war, at least with true states, has been eliminated as well. It is to the advantage of each state to forbid the injury of a citizen of a neighboring state just as strictly, to prevent it just as carefully, to exact the same compensation, and to punish it as severely as though it had been inflicted on a fellow citizen, if only to prevent thoughts of injury, plunder, and violence in its own citizens and to leave them no possibility for profit other than diligence and industry within the sphere designated by the law. This law about the security of neighbors is a necessary law of any state which is not a robber state. And this completely eliminates the possibility of any just complaint by one state against another and of every case of self-defense among nations. There are no necessary continuous direct relations of states as such with each other about which they might come to fight. As a rule there are only relations of the individual citizens of a state with the individual citizens of the other. A state could be injured only in the person of one of its citizens. But this injury is compensated on the spot, and thus the injured state is satisfied. Among such states there is no rank and sense of self-importance which could be offended or injured. No official is empowered to interfere in the internal affairs of a foreign state, nor can he be tempted to do so since he could not derive the slightest personal advantage from such interference. It is impossible for an entire nation to decide on a military invasion of a neighboring country for the sake of plunder, because in a state in which all are equal this plunder would not be the booty of a few but would have to be divided equally among all, and the share of each would never be enough to make war worth his while. Predatory war is possible and conceivable only where it is to the advantage of a few oppressors, while a numberless host of slaves has to put up with the disadvantages, the toil, and the cost. These true states will not need to fear that other states like them will make war on them. They need to fear only savages or barbarians whose lack of skill to prosper by work incited them to robbery, or slave nations whose masters might drive them out to plunder from which they themselves will never profit. The arts of culture will no doubt already have made each individual state stronger than the former, and it is to the common advantage of all states to strengthen themselves against the latter by alliance. No free state can reasonably tolerate constitutions next to it whose overlords derive any advantage from subjugating neighboring peoples and which therefore are a constant threat to the peace of their neighbors by their mere existence. A regard for their own security compels all free states to transform everyone around them into free states as well, and so, for the sake of their own well-being, to disseminate culture to savages and freedom to slave peoples in its vicinity. Soon the nations which they have cultivated or liberated will, with respect to those of their neighbors who are still barbarians or slaves, find themselves in the same situation in which only a short time ago states that had achieved freedom still earlier were with themselves, and they will be obliged to do for these neighbors what was done for them. And so, once only a few truly free states have come to be, the domain of culture and freedom, and with it universal peace, will gradually encompass the whole earth.

Justice in external relations of nations with each other and universal peace of states necessarily result in this way from the establishment of a just internal constitution and from securing peace among individuals. That establishment of a just internal constitution, however, and the liberation of the first nation to become truly free, necessarily result from the constantly growing pressure which the ruling classes exert on the ruled until it becomes unbearable. Such progress one may safely leave to the passions and blindness of those classes, even if they have been warned.

In this one true state all temptation to evil, indeed the very possibility of anyone's rationally deciding upon evil behavior, will be fully eliminated, and man will be given all possible encouragement to direct his will to the good.

No human being loves evil because it is evil. He loves in it only the advantages and enjoyments which evil promises and which in the present state of mankind it often really grants him. So long as this situation continues, so long as a premium is set upon vice, a fundamental improvement of humanity as a whole can hardly be hoped for. But in a civil constitution as it ought to be, as it is demanded by reason, as the thinker easily describes it, though he can as yet find it nowhere, and as it will necessarily be formed under the first people truly to achieve freedom—in such a constitution evil shows no advantages but rather the surest disadvantages, and the outbreak of self-love into unjust acts will be suppressed by self-love itself. Because of the unerring administration in such a state, every privilege and suppression of others, and each self-aggrandizement at another's expense will surely not only be in vain and a wasted effort, but will even turn against its author who will inevitably suffer the evil he had intended for another. There is no one *within* or *outside* his state nor on the whole earth whom he could injure with impunity. But it is not to be expected that anyone will intend evil merely to intend it even though he can never carry it out and nothing comes of it but his own loss. The use of freedom for evil is eliminated. Man must decide either to give up this freedom of his entirely and willingly become a passive wheel in the great machine of the whole, or to use this freedom for good. And so the good will then easily flourish on the soil prepared in this way. Once self-seeking intentions are no longer able to divide people and wear out their strength in fighting each other, nothing will be left to them other than to turn their united power against the one common opponent who still remains—recalcitrant, uncultivated nature. No longer divided by private purposes they will necessarily unite for the one common purpose and form a body animated throughout by the same spirit and the same love. Every disadvantage for an individual, since it can no longer be an advantage for anyone else, is now a disadvantage for the whole and for every individual member of the whole and will be felt by each member with equal pain and remedied with the same activity. Every advance made by a human being will be progress for all mankind. Here, where the small narrow self of persons has already been annihilated by the constitution, each will truly love every other as himself, as a component part of that great self which alone remains for his love and of which he too is nothing more than a mere component part that can only win or lose together with the whole. Here the resistance of evil to good has been eliminated, for evil can no longer occur. The quarrel of good people among themselves, even about the good, disappears, now that it has been made easier for them truly to love the good for its own sake and not for their own sake as the author thereof; now it can only matter to them that it occur, that truth be found, that the useful deed be done, but not through whom it may happen. Here everyone is always prepared to unite his strength with that of the other and to subordinate it to that of the other. All will support him who in the judgment of all can best accomplish the best, and all will with equal gladness enjoy his success.

This is the purpose of our earthly life which reason prescribes for us and the infallible achievement of which it guarantees. This is no goal for which we should strive merely to exercise our strength on something great but the reality of which we might perhaps have to give up. It shall, it must become real. This is a goal that must at some time be reached, as surely as there is a sensible world and a race of rational beings in time to whom nothing serious and rational is thinkable at all apart from this purpose and whose existence becomes intelligible only through this purpose. If the whole of human life is not to turn into a spectacle for a malicious spirit, which has implanted this inextinguishable yearning for the imperishable in poor humanity merely to find amusement in their repeated grasping for what incessantly eludes them, their ever repeated snatching at what will again elude their grasp, their restless running around an ever repeated circle, and to laugh at how seriously they take this tasteless farce; if the wise man, who will soon see through this game and be irked at continuing to play his part in it, is not to throw away his life and the moment of awakening to reason become the moment of earthly death—then that purpose has got to be achieved. Oh, it is achievable *in life* and *through life,* for reason commands me *to live.* It is achievable, for—I am.

III

But once it has been achieved and humanity has reached its goal, what will it do then? Beyond that condition there is no higher on earth. The generation which first has reached it can do nothing more than to persist in and vigorously maintain it, die, and leave offspring who will do the same as they have already done, and who in turn will leave offspring who do the same. Mankind would then have come to a halt on its path. Its earthly goal can, therefore, not be its highest goal. This earthly goal is understandable and attainable and finite. Even if we think of previous generations as means to the final, perfect one, we do not thereby escape the question of earnest reason: what does this final one exist for? Once human beings exist on earth they should, of course, not lead irrational lives but rational ones and become whatever they can on earth. But why should it exist at all, this human race, and why did it not equally well remain in the womb of nothingness? Reason is not there for the sake of existence, but existence for the sake of reason. An existence that does not in itself satisfy reason and answer all its questions cannot possibly be the true existence.

And then, are the acts commanded by the voice of conscience— that voice whose pronouncements I may not quibble about, but which I must silently obey—are these acts really the means and the only means for bringing about the earthly purpose of mankind? That I cannot but relate them to this purpose, and may not intend

them for any other purpose than this, is beyond question. But is my
intention always fulfilled? Does it take no more than to will the best
in order to make it happen? Oh, most good resolutions are completely lost for this world, and others seem even to work against the
purpose one had in mind for them. On the other hand, people's
most despicable passions, their vices, and their misdeeds very often
bring about the better more surely than the efforts of the righteous
person who never want to do evil so that good may result from it.
And it seems that the world's highest good grows and flourishes
quite independent of all human virtues and vices according to its
own law through an invisible and unknown power, just as the heav-
enly bodies follow their allotted course independent of all human
effort; and that this power carries with it all human intentions,
good and bad, in its own higher plan, and overwhelms what was
undertaken for other purposes and uses it for its own purpose.

So, even if the achievement of that earthly goal could be the
intention of our existence and if that would leave reason with no
questions, this purpose would not really be ours but the purpose of
that unknown power. We never know what promotes this purpose.
Nothing would be left to us except through our actions to give that
power some material no matter what, and to leave it to that power
to shape it according to its aim. It would be the highest wisdom not
to trouble ourselves about things that don't concern us, to live just
as we pleased, and be content to leave the outcome to that power.
Our inner moral law would be empty and superfluous and would
simply not befit a being which is incapable of more and is not
destined to something higher. To be at one with ourselves we would
have to refuse obedience to its voice and to suppress it as a perverted and foolish enthusiasm in us.

No, I will not refuse it obedience as surely as I live and exist. I
will obey it simply because it commands. Let this decision be the
first and highest in my mind, that by which everything else is directed but which is itself directed by or dependent upon nothing
else. Let it be the innermost principle of my spiritual life.

But as a rational being, which is already given a purpose through
its mere decision, I cannot act simply for nothing, for the sake of
nothing. If I am to be able to recognize that obedience as rational,

if it really is to be reason which forms my being, and not an extravagant fancy of my own invention or dragged in from somewhere or other which commands me to obey, then this obedience must have some outcome and serve some purpose or other. Evidently it does not serve the purpose of the natural earthly world. There must, therefore, be a supernatural world whose purpose it serves.

The fog of delusion clears from my eyes; I receive a new organ and with it a new world arises for me. It arises for me solely through the commandment of reason and connects only with that in my mind. I embrace this world—I suppose that, limited as I am by my senses, that is what I must call the unnameable—I embrace this world solely in the purpose and under the purpose which my obedience must have. It is nothing else at all but this necessary purpose itself which my reason adds to the comandment.

And how could I, apart from everything else, believe that this law is meant for the sensible world and that the whole purpose of the obedience it demands lies in that world, since that which alone is of importance in this obedience has no function at all in it, can never be a cause nor have consequences? In the sensible world which runs on the chain of material causes and effects, in which the result depends on what happened before, it is never a question of *how* an act was undertaken, *with what intentions and motives,* but only *what this act may be.*

If it were the whole intention of our existence to bring about an earthly condition of our species, then it would only require an infallible mechanism to determine our overt behaviour, and we would need to be nothing more than wheels which fit well into the whole machine. Freedom would then not only be in vain but it would even interfere, and the good will would be quite superfluous. The world would have been arranged most clumsily and would proceed toward its goal wastefully and circuitously. It would have been better, mightly world spirit, had you taken away this freedom, which you have to fit into your plans with difficulty only and through another arrangement, and had straightway compelled us to act as we should for your plans. You would then reach your goal by the shortest road, as the least of the inhabitants of your worlds can tell you. But I am free. And therefore such a connection of causes and effects, in which freedom is absolutely superfluous and pointless, cannot exhaust my whole vocation. I am meant to be free. For it is not the mechanically produced act which constitutes our true worth, but only the free determination of freedom solely for the sake of the commandment and for no other purpose at all. This is what the inner voice of conscience tells us. The bond with which the law binds me is a bond for living minds. It disdains to rule over dead mechanism and only addresses itself to the living and self-active. It demands this obedience. This obedience cannot be superfluous.

And with this the eternal world rises more brightly before me and the basic law of its order stands clearly before my mind's eye. In it *the will*, as it lies hidden from all mortal eyes in the secret darkness of my heart, is the pure and sole first link in a chain of consequences which runs through the entire invisible realm of spirits, just as in the earthly world *the act*, a certain movement of matter, becomes the first link in a material chain which flows through the whole system of matter. The will is what is effective and alive in the world of reason, just as motion is what is effective and alive in the world of sense. I stand at the midpoint between two directly opposed worlds: a visible world in which the act is decisive, and an invisible incomprehensible world in which the will is decisive. I am one of the original powers for both worlds. It is my will that embraces both. This will is already in and for itself a component of the supersensible world. As I move it through some decision I move and change something in that world and my efficacy flows out over the whole and brings forth something new and everlasting which then exists and does not need to be made again. This will breaks out in a material act and this act belongs to the world of sense and does there what it can do.

I will not gain entry into the supernatural world only after I have been severed from connection with the earthly one. I already am and live in it now, far more truly than in the earthly. Already now it is my only firm standpoint, and eternal life, which I have already long since taken possession of, is the only reason why I still care to carry on my life on earth. Heaven, as it is called, does not lie beyond the grave. It already surrounds us here and its light is kindled in every pure heart. My will is mine, and it is the only thing which is entirely mine and completely depends upon me, and through it I am even now a citizen of the realm of freedom and rational self-activity. What determination of my will—the only thing through which I reach out of the dust into this realm—will fit into its order I am at every moment told by my conscience, the bond by which that world unceasingly holds me and connects me with itself. And it depends entirely upon me to give myself the bidden determination. I then cultivate myself for this world, and therefore work in and for it in that I cultivate one of its members. In it, and only in it, do I pursue my purpose, without vacillation or doubt according to a fixed rule, sure of success since no alien power opposes my will there. That in the world of the senses my will, so far as it really is will, as it should be, also becomes an act, is only the law of this sensible world. I did not want the act as I wanted the will. Only the latter was wholly and purely my work, and it was also all that came purely from myself. There was no need for a further special act on my part to connect the act to it. It connected itself to my will according to the law of the second world to which I am related through my will and in which this will is likewise an original power, as in the first.

Of course, when I regard my will, subject to the dictates of conscience, as act, as efficient cause in the world of the senses, I have to relate it as a means to that earthly purpose of humanity. Not as though I would then first have to survey the world plan and calculate by that insight what I have to do. Rather, the particular action directly commanded to me by conscience at once presents itself to me as that through which alone I, in my situation, can contribute toward the attainment of that purpose. Even if after the act it should seem to me that the purpose was not furthered by it, or even that it had been hindered, I cannot for that reason regret the act, I cannot become confused about it in my own mind so long as I only obeyed my conscience in performing it. Whatever consequences it may have for this world, nothing but good can result from it for another world. And even for this world my conscience, precisely because it seems to have missed its purpose, now bids me to repeat the act more effectively; or, because it seems to have hindered its purpose, to remove what is detrimental and abolish what prevents success. I will as I ought, and the new act results. It may happen that the consequences of this new act in the world of sense seem to me no better than those of the first. But I remain just as calm about them in respect to the other world, and for the present one I am now obliged to improve by new efforts what I previously did. And so, even should it always seem that throughout my entire earthly life I do not advance the good in this world by a hair's breadth, I may nevertheless not give it up. After every failed step I must believe that the next one may yet succeed. For that other world, however, no step is lost.

In short, I don't promote the earthly purpose just for its own sake and as a final end, but because my true final end, obedience to the law, does not present itself otherwise to me in the present world than as the promotion of that purpose. I could give it up if only I could ever refuse obedience to the law, or if ever in this life the law could present itself to me other than as a commandment to promote this purpose within my situation. I will really have given it up in another life in which the commandment will set me another purpose which is quite incomprehensible down here. In this life I must *want* to promote it because I have to obey. Whether the act that results from this lawful willing *really promotes* it is not my concern. I am responsible only for the *will*, which down here can, of course, aim only at the earthly purpose, but not for the consequences. Prior to the act I can never give up this purpose. But I can certainly give up the act after I have done it, and repeat or improve it. According to my most authentic being and most intimate purpose I am thus already living and working here only for the other world, and the efficiency for this other world is the only one of which I am quite sure. I work for the sensible world only for the sake of the other one, and this because I cannot work for the other one at all without at least *wanting* to work for this one.

I want to establish myself firmly and come to feel at home in this, for me, quite new view of my vocation. The present life cannot reasonably be thought of as the whole purpose of my existence or of the existence of mankind in general. There is something in me and something is demanded of me which finds no application in this whole life and which is utterly pointless and superfluous for the highest which can be produced on earth. Man must, therefore, have a purpose which lies beyond this life. If, however, the present life, which is nonetheless laid on him, and which can[3] only be meant for the development of reason, since the already awakened reason bids us to preserve it and to promote its highest purpose with all our strength—if this life is not to be wholly in vain and useless in the series of our existence, then it must at least relate to a future life as means to end. Now, there is nothing in this present life whose final consequences do not remain on earth, nothing by which it might be connected with a life to come other than the good will, which in turn bears no intrinsic fruit in this world because of the fundamental law of this world. It can only be, it must be, the good will through which we work for another life and for the immediate goal thereof which is only there first to be set up for us. It is the, to us, invisible consequences of this good will through which we first acquire a firm standpoint in that life, from which we can then progress further in it.

That our good will in and for and through itself must have consequences we already know in this life, for reason cannot command anything pointless. But *what* these consequences may be and how it may even be possible for a mere will to have an effect, about that we cannot even think anything as long as we are still caught up in this material world, and it is wisdom not to undertake an investigation of which we can already know in advance that it will fail. In respect of the nature of these consequences then, the present life, in relation to a future[4] one, is a life *in faith.* In the future life we will possess these consequences, for we will proceed from them with our activity and build on them. This other life, in relation to the consequences of our good will in the present one, will therefore be a life of *seeing.* In this other life we will also have an immediate goal

3. [I have read '*das nicht lediglich*' as an error for '*das lediglich.*' The edition of 1845 prepared by Fichte's son Immanuel Hermann Fichte drops the '*nicht.*' The recent Bavarian Academy Edition retains it, but queries it.]

4. [Here Fichte refers to the next life as '*ein künftiges Leben.*' Later, when he asserts that it is not in the future but is already present, he refers to it as '*ein zukünftiges Leben.*' English does not have two words for '*future*' which might signal his point that the life to come is not in the future of our present time.]

set up for that life, as we had in the present one; for we must continue to be active. But we remain finite beings, and for finite beings every activity is a particular one; and a particular act has a particular goal. As the world we find in the present life, the practical arrangement of this world for the work we have to do, the culture and benevolence among men which has already been reached, and our own sensory powers are related to the goal of this life: so the consequences of our good will in the present life will relate in the future life to the goal of that life. The present life is the beginning of our existence. We have been adequately equipped for it and given a firm footing in it as a free gift. The future life is the continuation of this existence. For it we must ourselves earn a beginning and a definite standpoint.

And now the present life no longer seems useless and in vain. It has been given us in order to win this firm foundation in the future life, and for that alone. And only through this foundation is the present life connected with our whole eternal existence. It is quite possible that the immediate goal of this second life will, with certainty and according to a rule, be just as unattainable to a being with finite strength as is the goal of the present life, and that there the good will may also seem to be superfluous and pointless. But it can be lost there just as little as it can here, for it is the necessarily enduring commandment of reason, from which it cannot be separated. Its necessary efficacy would in this case, therefore, direct us to a third life in which the consequences of the good will from the second life would show themselves, and which subsequent life would also only be *believed* in this second life; believed though, with firmer and more unshakable confidence, once we had already experienced in fact the veracity of reason and found the fruits of a pure heart in one already completed life faithfully preserved in another.

As in the present life we come by our concept of a particular goal only through the commandment of a particular act, and our whole intuition of the given sensible world only comes to be through this concept, just so the concept of an immediate goal of a future life will be based on a similar commandment which at present is completely unthinkable to us, and this concept will be the basis of the intuition of a world in which the consequences of our good will in the present life will be advanced to us. The present world exists for us at all only through the commandment of duty. The other will likewise come to be for us only through another commandment of duty. For in no other way does a world exist for a rational being.

This, therefore, is my whole sublime vocation, my true being. I am a member of two orders. One purely spiritual, in which I exist through the bare pure will; and one sensible in which I act through my deed. The whole final purpose of reason is its own pure activity, simply through itself and without needing an instrument outside of itself, i.e., independence from everything which is not itself reason, absolutely unconditioned being. The will is the living principle of reason, is reason itself, if reason is conceived purely and independently. That reason is active through itself means that pure will, merely as such, is active and present. Only infinite reason lives immediately and solely in this purely spiritual order. The finite individual, who is not the rational world itself but only one among many of its members, necessarily lives at the same time in a sensible order, that is, in one which presents him with still another goal besides pure rational activity: with a material purpose to be promoted with instruments and powers which, to be sure, are directly subject to the will, but whose efficacy is also conditioned by their own natural laws. Yet, as surely as reason is reason, the will must act simply through itself, independent of the natural laws by which the act is determined. And that is why every finite being's sensible life points to a higher one into which the will may conduct him merely through itself, and in which it may secure him a place—a place, of course, which will again present itself to us in a sensible way, as a *state of things,* and not at all as a mere will.

These two orders, the purely spiritual and the sensible, which latter may consist of an innumerable series of particular lives, are in me and run parallel to each other from the first moment an active reason is developed in me. The latter order is only an appearance for myself and for those who find themselves in the same life with me; the former alone gives meaning, purpose, and value to the latter. I *am* immortal, imperishable, eternal as soon as I decide to obey the law of reason; I must not first *become* so. The supersensible world is no future world; it is present. It can be no more present at one point of finite existence than at another. It can be no more present after an existence of myriads of lifetimes than at this moment. Other determinations of my *sensible* existence are future, but these are the true life just as little as the present determination. In that decision I take hold of eternity and strip off life in the dust and all other sensible lives which might still await me, and place myself far above them. I become for myself the sole source of all my being and my appearances; and from now on I have life in myself unconditioned by anything outside myself. My will, which I myself and no stranger align with the order of that world, is this source of true life and of eternity.

But it is also only my will which is this source. Only by recognizing this will as the authentic seat of moral goodness, and by really elevating it to that goodness, do I receive the certainty and possession of that supersensible world.

I ought to will in conformity with the law without regard to any intelligible and apparent purpose, without investigating whether anything other than the willing itself may result from my willing. My will stands alone, separate from everything which is not itself. It is its own world for itself and merely through itself; not just so that it may be the absolutely *first* and that *before* it there be no other link that may connect with it and determine it, but also that no thinkable and intelligible *second* may result from it and thereby have its activity fall under an alien law. Were a second to proceed from it, and from that a third, etc., in a sensible world we can conceive opposed to the spiritual world, then its strength would be broken by the resistance of the independent elements in that world which would have to be set in motion; its mode of activity would no longer fully correspond to the purpose expressed in the volition, and the will would not remain free but would in part be limited by the laws peculiar to its heterogeneous sphere of activity.

In the present sensible world, which is the only one known to me, I must really take that view of the will. Of course, I still have to believe (that is, act as though I thought) that my tongue, my hand, my foot could be set in motion by my volition. But how a mere breath such as the will, a pressure of the intelligence upon itself, could be a principle of motion in the heavy earthly mass, about that I cannot only think nothing, but even the mere claim is sheer nonsense before the judgment seat of the observing understanding. In this field the motion of matter, even in myself, must be explained purely by the inner forces of bare matter.

A view of my will, however, such as I have described, I do not attain just by becoming persuaded that it is not merely the highest active principle for this world—which it surely could become without proper freedom through the mere influence of the whole world system, much as we have to conceive the formative force in nature—but rather, that it simply disdains all earthly purposes and in general all purposes lying outside it, and establishes itself for its own sake as the final purpose. But solely by such a view of my will am I referred to a supersensible order in which the will becomes a cause purely through itself, without any implements outside it, in a sphere which like itself is purely spiritual and throughout penetrable by it.

That lawful willing is demanded simply for its own sake—a piece of information which I can only find as a fact in my inner being and which can come to me in no other way—this was the first step in my thinking. The second step in my thinking was that this demand is rational and the source and guideline of everything else which is rational, that it takes its direction from nothing else, but that everything else takes its direction from that demand and has to depend on it—a conviction to which I also cannot attain from the outside but only inwardly through the unshakable assent I freely accord to that demand. And these steps first led me to believe in a supersensible eternal world. If I remove those steps then that world ceases to be an issue. Many people say and assume without further proof as self-evident, and praise as the height of the wisdom of life, that all human virtue must always have a particular external purpose in view and must first be sure of the attainability of this purpose before it can act and before it can be virtue. This would imply that reason does not contain within itself a principle and guideline of its activity but would first have to receive this guideline from the outside through observation of a world alien to it. If what these people say were true then the ultimate purpose of our existence would be down here on earth; human nature would be fully exhausted and thoroughly explainable by our earthly vocation, and there would be no rational reason for extending our thoughts beyond the present life.

But what I have just said to myself can be said and taught by any thinker who has accepted those first steps historically from somewhere or other, perhaps because of a craving for the new and unusual, and who can reason correctly from them. He will then present to us the manner of thought of an alien life, not of his own. Everything will drift by him empty and meaningless because he lacks the sense with which to apprehend its reality. He is a blind man who, having historically learned a few true propositions about colors, has constructed a perfectly correct theory of them, even though color does not exist for him. He can say how it *would have to be* under certain conditions, but it *is* not so for him because he does not exist under those conditions. The sense with which to apprehend the eternal life is acquired only by actually giving up and sacrificing the sensuous and its purposes for the law, which lays claim only to our will and not our deeds; by giving it up with the firm conviction that this is rational and the only rational thing to do. Only through this renunciation of the earthly does faith in the eternal come forth in our soul and is established in isolation as the only support to which we can still hold after we have given up everything else, as the one animating principle which still lifts our bosom and still inspires our life. In the imagery of a sacred doctrine, one must first die to the world and be born again, to be able to enter the kingdom of God.

I see, oh I now see clearly before me, the reason for my former negligence and blindness in spiritual matters. Filled with earthly purposes and lost in them with all our thought and attention, set in motion and driven only by the idea of a result to be achieved outside us, by the desire for this result and the pleasure of it, insensible and dead to the pure impulse of reason which gives laws to itself and assigns us a purely spiritual purpose, the immortal Psyche remains tethered to the earth with her pinions bound. Our philosophy becomes the history of our own heart and life, and as we find ourselves to be, so we think in general of man and his vocation. Never driven otherwise than by the desire for what can be realized in this world, there is for us no true freedom, no freedom which would have the ground of its determination absolutely and fully within itself. Our freedom is at most that of the self-forming plant; not essentially higher but only more artful in its results; producing not a material form with roots, leaves, and blossoms, but a mind with drives, thoughts, and acts. Of true freedom we are unable to perceive anything whatever because we are not in possession of it. When there is talk of it we drag the words down to our meaning or curtly and firmly dismiss such talk as nonsense. If we lose the knowledge of freedom we also lose the sense for another world. Everything of this kind passes us by like words not addressed to us at all, like an ashen grey shadow without color or meaning which we are unable to seize and hold fast at any point. Without being in the least interested we leave everything as it is. Or, if a more eager zeal ever impels us to consider such things seriously, we see clearly and can prove that all those ideas are untenable and empty extravagances which the informed person dismisses. And, given the presuppositions from which we proceed and which are taken from our own innermost experience, we are completely right, and are irrefutable and unteachable so long as we remain who we are. The excellent doctrines about freedom, duty, and eternal life, which are accorded special authority among our people, are transformed for us into adventurous fables, similar to those of Tartarus and the Elysian fields, without any exact disclosure of our true sentiments, since we find it advisable to use these images to maintain public decorum among the uneducated; or, if we are less given to thought ourselves and still fettered by the bonds of authority, we ourselves sink to the level of the uneducated, in that we believe what, *understood in that way*, would only be a silly fable, and find, in those purely spiritual indications, the promise of continuing into all eternity the same miserable existence which we lead down here.

In a word: only through the fundamental improvement of my will do I come to see my existence and my vocation in a new light. Without it there is vain darkness in me and around me, however much I may ponder, and no matter with what excellent mental gifts I may be equipped. Only the improvement of the heart leads to true wisdom. Now then, may my whole life flow unceasingly toward this one purpose!

IV

My lawful will, merely as such, in and through itself, is to have consequences, surely and without exception. Every dutiful determination of my will, even if no act resulted from it, is to have an effect in another world which is incomprehensible to me, and apart from this dutiful determination of the will nothing is to have an effect there. What am I thinking when I think this? What do I presuppose?

Evidently a *law*, a rule simply valid without exception according to which the dutiful will must have consequences. Just as in this earthly world which surrounds me I assume a law according to which this ball, if pushed in this particular direction with this particular force by my hand, will necessarily move in that direction with a particular measure of speed, and will perhaps push another ball with this measure of force, which will then itself move on with a particular speed, and so on indefinitely. As here, in the mere direction and movement of my hand, I already know and apprehend all the consequent directions and movements with the same certainty as though I perceived them already present before me, just so I apprehend in my dutiful will a series of necessary and inevitable consequences in the spiritual world as though they were already present. Only that I cannot determine them like the consequences in the material world, that is, I only know *that* they will be, but not *how* they will be. And when I do that, I think a *law* of the spiritual world in which my pure will is one of the motive forces, just as my hand is one of the motive forces in the material world. That firmness of my confidence and the thought of this law of a spiritual world are fully one and the same; not two thoughts, one of which would be mediated by the other, but the very same thought; just as the certainty with which I count on a particular movement and the thought of a mechanical law of nature are the same. The concept "law" expresses nothing other than reason's firm and unshakable adherence to a principle and the absolute impossibility of assuming the contrary.

I assume such a law of a spiritual world, which is not given by my will nor by the will of any finite being nor by the will of all finite beings taken together, but to which my will and the will of all finite beings are themselves subject. Neither I nor any finite, and therefore in some way sensuous, being can at all comprehend how a mere pure will can have consequences and what these consequences might be like, since it is the essence of their finitude not to be able to comprehend that; and that while the bare will as such is fully within their control, its consequences will necessarily be seen as sensible conditions owing to their sensible nature. How, then, could I or any other finite being take something we simply can neither think nor comprehend, set it up as our purpose, and thereby give it reality?

I cannot say that the natural law of motion in the material world is given by my hand, or by any body at all which is part of this world and determined by the universal fundamental law of gravity. This body is itself subject to this natural law and can move another body only according to this law and so far as in consequence of that law it participates in the general motive force in nature. Just as little does a finite will give the law to the supersensible world which no finite mind can encompass. All finite wills, rather, are subject to the law of that world and can produce something in it only so far as this law already exists and so far as they submit to its condition and enter into the sphere of its efficacy through a sense of duty according to the fundamental law of that world for finite wills. Through a sense of duty, I say—the only bond which ties them to that world, the sole nerve which descends from it to them, the only means by which they can have a reciprocal effect in it. As the universal force of attraction holds all bodies and unites them with it and with each other, and as only if it is presupposed does movement of individual bodies become possible, so does that supersensible law unite and contain and subsume under itself, all finite rational beings.

My will, and the will of all finite beings, may be seen from a double point of view: partly as mere *volition*, an inner action upon itself, and to that extent the will is complete in itself and self-enclosed by the mere act; and partly as *something*, as a *fact*. This latter is what it is for me initially, so far as I regard it as complete. But it should become this outside of me as well; in the *sensible world* as motive principle of my hand, for example, from whose movement other movements result; in the *supersensible world*, as principle of a series of spiritual consequences of which I have no conception. Seen in the first way, as mere act, it is fully under my control. But that it becomes the second at all, and becomes it as first principle, does not depend on me but on a law to which I myself am subject, the law of nature in the sensible world, and a supersensible law in the supersensible world.

What kind of a law of the spiritual world is this that I'm thinking of? For I am anxious only to explain and analyze this concept,

which is there now, firm and formed, and to which I neither can
nor may add anything. Evidently it is like no law in my sensible
world, or any other possible sensible world, to which something
would be presupposed other than a mere will, to which an *enduring
passive being* would be presupposed, from which an inner force is
released through the impulse, perhaps, of a will. For—this is after
all the content of my faith—my will is to act simply through itself,
without any instrument to weaken its expression, in a sphere fully
commensurate with it, act as reason upon reason, as spirit upon
spirit; in a sphere to which it would, however, not give the law of
life, of activity, of continuity, but which would contain this law within itself. As reason, therefore, it would act upon *self-active* reason.
But self-active reason is will. The law of the supersensible world
would therefore be a *will*.

A will which acts purely and solely as will, through itself, entirely
without any instrument of sensible material upon which to act,
which absolutely through itself is at once *deed* and *product*, whose
willing is occurrence, whose commanding is execution; in which
therefore the demand of reason to be absolutely free and self-active
is realized. A will which is in itself law, which does not determine
itself by moods and caprice, by prior deliberation and considering
back and forth, but which is determined eternally and unalterably,
and on which one can surely and unfailingly count, just as we
mortals surely count on the laws of our world. A will in which the
lawful will of finite beings has consequences without fail; but only
their lawful will, since nothing else will move it and everything else
is as good as nonexistent for it.

That sublime will, therefore, does not go its own way separate
from the rest of the rational world. Between it and all finite rational
beings there is a spiritual bond, and it itself is this spiritual bond of
the world of reason. I purely and resolutely will my duty, and It
then wills that I succeed, at least in the spiritual world. Each lawful
resolution of the will of a finite being enters into that sublime will
and, to speak our language, moves and determines it, not in consequence of a momentary pleasure, but in consequence of the eternal
law of its being. The thought which formerly was still shrouded in
darkness for me now comes before my soul with surprising clarity,
the thought that my will has consequences merely as will and

through itself. It has consequences in that it is unfailingly and directly perceived by another will related to it, which itself is deed and the sole principle of life of the spiritual world. It has its first consequence *in that will*, and only *through* it does it have an effect on the rest of the spiritual world, which everywhere is nothing but a product of that infinite will.

So I flow—mortals have to use words of their language—so I flow into that will; and it is the voice of conscience within me, which in every situation of my life teaches me what I have to do, through which It in turn influences me.[5] That voice is the oracle from the eternal world, made sensuous only by my surroundings and translated only by my perception into my language, which announces to me how I for my part must adapt myself to the order of the spiritual world or to infinite will which itself is the order of this spiritual world. I neither survey nor see through that spiritual order, and do not need to. I am only a link in its chain, and can judge the whole just as little as a single tone of a song can judge the harmony of the whole. But I must know what I myself ought to be in this harmony of spirits; for only I can make myself into that, and it is directly revealed to me by a voice which comes to me from that world. In this way I am connected with the One *which is there*, and take part in its being. There is nothing truly real, lasting, imperishable in me except these two parts: the voice of my conscience and my free obedience. Through the first the spiritual world bends down to me and embraces me as one of its members; through the second I raise myself into this world, grasp it, and act in it. That infinite will, however, is the mediator between it and me; for it is itself the original source of it and of me. This is the one thing that is true and imperishable, toward which my soul moves from its innermost depth; all else is mere appearance which disappears and reappears in a new semblance.

This will unites me with itself; it unites me with all finite beings like me and is the general mediator between all of us. That is the

---

5. Fichte's unidiomatic construct *"einfließen auf"* is halfway between "flow into" and "have an influence on." I chose to favor one meaning at the beginning of the sentence and the other meaning at the end of the sentence.]

great secret of the invisible world and its fundamental law so far as it is a *world* or *a system of a number of individual wills: that union and direct interaction of a number of autonomous and independent wills with each other;* a secret which already in the present life lies clearly open to everyone's view without anyone noticing it or bothering to wonder about it. The voice of conscience, which imposes his particular duty on each, is the ray of light on which we come forth from the infinite and are established as individual and particular beings; it draws the limits of our personality; it, therefore, is our true original component, the ground and stuff of our whole life. The absolute freedom of the will, which we likewise bring with us from the infinite down into the world of time, is the principle of this our life. I act. If we presuppose the sensible intuition through which alone I become a personal intelligence, it will be easy to understand how I must necessarily know of this, my action. I know it because I myself am the one who is acting. It can be understood how by means of this sensible intuition my mental *acting* appears to me as a *deed in a sensible world,* and on the other hand how, through the same sensualization, the commandment of duty, which in itself is purely spiritual, should appear to me as a *commandment of such a deed.* It can be understood how an objective world, as precondition of this deed and partly as its consequence and product, should appear to me. With this I always remain only *in myself* and in my own domain. Whatever exists for me is developed purely and solely out of my self. Everywhere I intuit only myself and no alien true being outside of me.

But in this my world I also assume the activity of other beings who are supposed to be independent of me and autonomous just like me. How these beings can know for themselves of the actions which proceed from them can be understood: they know of them in the same way I know of mine. But how *I* can know of them is simply incomprehensible, just as it is incomprehensible how *they* can know of my existence and of my activities, which knowledge I do after all ascribe to them. How do they enter my world, and I theirs, since the principle according to which the consciousness of ourselves and our activities and of their sensible conditions is developed out of ourselves, the principle that every intelligence must indisputably know what it is doing—since this principle simply does not apply here? How are free spirits informed about free spirits, now that we know that free spirits alone are real, and that an independent, sensible world through which they might act upon each other is quite unthinkable? Or do you want to tell me that you perceive rational beings like yourself through the changes they bring about in the sensible world? Then I ask you in turn how you can perceive these changes themselves. I understand very well how you perceive changes produced by the mere mechanism of nature; for the law of this mechanism is nothing other than the law of your own thought according to which you further develop the world you have all at once posited. But the changes we are here talking about are not supposed to be brought about by the mechanism of nature, but by a free will elevated above all nature, and only so far as you see them that way do you infer free beings like yourself from them. What, then, would be the law in you by which you could develop the determinations of other wills absolutely independent of you? In short, this mutal knowledge and interaction of free beings already in this world is quite incomprehensible according to laws of nature and of thought, and is explainable only through the One in which they hang together, though for themselves they are separated, through the infinite will which keeps and supports all in its sphere. The knowledge which we have of each other does not flow directly from you to me and from me to you. For ourselves we are separated by an insurmountable barrier. We know of each other only through our common spiritual source. Only in it do we come to know each other and act upon each other. The inner voice of that will, which speaks to me only so far as it imposes duties upon me, calls to me: here respect the image of freedom on earth, here a work which bears its imprint. And this alone is the principle through which I recognize you and your work, in that conscience commands me to respect it.

Where, then, do our feelings come from and our sensible intuition and our discursive laws of thought, which all form the basis of the sensible world we see and in which we believe that we influence each other? To answer in respect of the latter two, intuition and the laws of thought, that they are the laws of reason in and for itself, is not to give a satisfactory answer. For us, of course, who are limited to the domain of these laws, it is even impossible to think of other laws, or of a reason which would be subject to other laws. But the true law of reason in itself is only the practical law, the law of the supersensible world, or that sublime will. And, if we can set that aside for a moment, how do we account for our general agreement about *feelings,* which after all are something positive, immediate, and inexplicable? But that we all see the same sensible world depends on this agreement about feeling, intuition, and laws of thought.

This is a correspondent incomprehensible limitation of the finite rational beings of our species, and just in this, that they are correspondingly limited, do they become one species. So answers the philosophy of bare pure knowledge, and must stop with this as its final anwer. But what could limit reason other than *what itself is reason,* and limit all finite reason other than infinite reason? This agreement of us all about the underlying sensible world given, as it were, in advance, as the sphere of our duty—which if looked at carefully, is just as incomprehensible as our agreement about the products of our reciprocal freedom—this agreement is brought about by the One Eternal Infinite Will. Our belief in this world, which I considered above, as belief in our duty, is really faith in It, in Its reason, in Its fidelity.[6] What then is the really and purely true which we assume in the sensible world and in which we believe? Nothing other than that the faithful and sincere fulfillment of duty in this world will produce a life into all eternity promoting our freedom and morality. If this occurs, then our world has truth, the only truth possible for finite beings. It must occur, for this world is the result of the eternal will in us; but this will can, because of the laws of its being, have no other final purpose for finite beings than the one indicated.

That eternal will is thus surely the creator of the world, in the only way in which it can be and in which alone a creation is required: *in finite reason.* Those who would have it build a world out of eternal inert matter, which then, too, could be only inert and lifeless, like artifacts built by human hands and no eternal process of a development out of itself, or those who think they can conceive the emergence of a material something from nothing, know neither the world nor that Will. There is Nothing anywhere if matter alone is to be something, and everywhere and to all eternity Nothing re-

6. [The allusion to the God of traditional religion is even stronger in German where both "God" and "will" take the same personal pronoun.]

mains. Only reason is; infinite reason in itself, and finite reason in it and through it. Only in our minds does it create a world, or at least that *from* which and *through* which we produce it: the call to duty; and concordant feelings, intuition, and laws of thought. It is *its* light through which we see light and all that appears to us in this light. In our minds *it continues to build* this world and intervenes in it in that it intervenes in our minds through the call of duty as soon as another free being changes something in this world. In our minds it *maintains* this world and thereby our finite existence of which alone we are capable, in that it constantly produces further conditions from our conditions. After it has, in accordance with its higher purpose, tested us sufficiently for our next destiny, and we will have made ourselves ready for that destiny, it will annihilate our present life[7] with what we call death and introduce us into a new life, the product of our dutiful activity in the present life. All our life is Its life. We are in Its hand and remain there, and no one can tear us out of it. We are eternal because It is.

Sublime living Will, which no name can name and no concept encompass, well may I elevate my mind to you; for you and I are not separate. Your voice sounds in me and mine resounds in you, and all my thoughts, if only they are true and good, are thought in you. In you, the incomprehensible, I myself and the world become completely comprehensible to me, all puzzles of my existence are solved, and the most perfect harmony arises in my spirit.

Childlike simplicity, devoted to you, apprehends you best. A person of such simplicity believes that you know and see through his innermost heart, are the ever-present faithful witness of his sentiments who alone knows of his sincerity and who alone knows him even when he is misunderstood by the whole world. He believes you to be the father who always means well and who will direct all to the best. To your benevolent decisions he gives himself up body and soul. Do with me what you will, he says, I know that it will be good as surely as it is *you* who do it. The pondering understanding which has only heard of you but has never seen you, wants to teach us to know your intrinsic nature and presents us with a contradictory monstrosity which it gives out to be your image, ridiculous to the

---

7. [Fichte writes *"dieselbe,"* which here must refer to that next destiny. But I feel sure that this is a mistake and have made what I considered the appropriate change.]

mere understanding, hateful and repulsive to the wise and good.

Before you I cover my face and put my hand over my mouth. How you are for yourself and appear to yourself I can never understand as surely as I can never become you. After having lived through a thousand times a thousand spirit-lives I will still comprehend you just as little as I do now in this hut of earth. What I comprehend becomes finite through my mere comprehension, and the finite can never be transformed into the infinite even through an infinite increase and enhancement. You differ from the finite not in degree but in kind. Through that increase they only make you into a greater human being, and always into a greater, but never into God, the infinite, who is beyond all measure. I only have this discursively progressing consciousness and can conceive of no other. How might I ascribe this to you? There are limits in the concept of personality. How could I apply it to you without those limitations?

I don't want to try something made impossible for me by the nature of finitude and which would be of no use to me. I don't want to know how you are in yourself. But if I become what I ought to be, then your relations and connections with me, the finite, and to all finite beings, lie open to my eyes and surround me with brighter clarity than the consciousness of my own existence. You *produce* in me the knowledge of my duty, of my vocation in the ranks of rational beings; *how,* I neither know nor need to know. You *know and discern* what I think and want; *how* you can know, through what act *you* bring about this consciousness, of that I understand nothing. I even know very well that the concept of an act, and of a particular act of conciousness, applies only to me but not to you, the infinite one. You *will,* because you will that my free obedience have consequences into all eternity; the act of your will I do not comprehend; I only know this much, that it is not similar to mine. You *act,* and your will itself is the deed; but the manner of your acting is directly opposed to the manner which alone I can conceive. You *live and are,* for you know, will, and act ever present to finite reason; but *you* are not as, through all eternity, I can alone conceive a being.

In the contemplation of these your relations to me, the finite being, I will rest content. I know immediately only what I ought to do. This I want to do sincerely, gladly, and without quibbling; for it is your will that commands it, the part assigned to me by the spiritual world plan; and the strength with which I carry it out is your strength. What is commanded by that voice and carried out with this strength is certainly and truly good in that plan. I remain calm among all the events of the world, for they are in *your* world. Nothing can perplex me or estrange or dishearten me, as surely as you live and I see your life. For in you and through you, oh infinite one, I see even my present world in a different light. 'Nature' and 'nature's course' in the destinies and activities of free beings become empty and meaningless words next to you. There is no longer any nature; you, only you, exist.

It no longer seems to me the final purpose of the present world that a state of universal peace among men and their unconditional control of the mechanism of nature be produced merely for its own sake, but rather that it be produced by human beings themselves. And, since it is meant for all, that it be produced by all as one great free moral community. The fundamental law of the great moral realm, of which the present life is a part, is: nothing new and better for the individual, except through his dutiful will; nothing new and better for the community, except through the communal dutiful will. That is why the good will of the individual is so often lost for this world, because it is still only that of the individual, and the will of the majority does not agree with it; and its consequences fall only into a future world. That is why even the passions and vices of people seem to contribute to the attainment of a better world; *not in and for themselves;* in this sense good can never come of evil, but rather in that they balance the opposed vices and finally through their greater weight, destroy them and therewith themselves at the same time. Oppression could never have gained the upper hand if cowardice, baseness, and mutual mistrust among people had not paved the way for it. Oppression will increase until it eliminates cowardice and the slavish attitude, and despair reawakens lost courage. Then the two opposed vices will have destroyed each other and the noblest in all human relations, lasting freedom, will have issued from them.

Strictly speaking the acts of free beings have consequences only upon other free beings: for in these and for these alone is there a world. The world is just that about which all agree. But they have consequences in them only through the infinite will which mediates

all individuals. But a call, a proclamation of this will to us, is always
a summons to a particular duty. So even that in the world which we
call evil, the consequence of the misuse of freedom, exists only
through *it;* and this consequence exists for all for whom it exists
only in that duties are imposed upon them by it. Were it not in the
eternal plan of our moral education and the education of mankind
that just these duties should have been imposed on us, they would
not be imposed on us, and that through which they are imposed on
us, which we call evil, would not have happened at all. To this
extent everything that *happens* is good and absolutely purposeful.
Only one world is possible, a thoroughly good one. Everything that
occurs in this world serves to the improvement and education of
human beings, and through this to bringing about their earthly
goal. This higher world plan is what we call nature when we say:
nature leads man to industry through want, through the evils of
general disorder to a just constitution, through the hardships of
their constant wars to final eternal peace. Your will, infinite one,
your providence alone is this higher nature.

Artless simplicity also grasps this best when it recognizes this life
as a testing ground and educational institution, as a school for
eternity; when in any fate which befalls it, the most trivial as well as
the most weighty, it sees your dispositions which are to lead it to
good; when it firmly believes that all things must be for the best for
those who love their duty and know you.

Oh, surely I have spent the past days of my life in darkness;
surely I have built error upon error and deemed myself wise. Only
now do I fully understand the doctrine which from your lips
seemed so strange to me, wonderful spirit, even though my understanding could find no fault in it; for only now do I see it to its full
extent, in its deepest depths, and in all its implications.

Man is not a product of the sensible world, and the final purpose
of his existence cannot be attained in it. His vocation goes beyond
time and space and everything sensible. He must know what he is
and what he is to make of himself. As his vocation is lofty, so his
thought too must be able to rise entirely above all limits of sensibility. He must have an obligation to this; where his being is at
home, there necessarily his thought will also be at home. And the

most truly human view which alone is appropriate to him and
presents his whole power of thought is the view through which he
rises above those limits and through which the whole sensible world
is transformed for him purely into nothingness, into a mere reflection in mortal eyes of the nonsensible, which alone exists.

Many have been raised to this view without artificial thinking,
merely through their great heart and their purely moral instinct,
because they lived primarily only with the heart and in feeling.
With their behavior they denied the agency and reality of the sensible world and let it count for nothing in reaching their decisions
and formulating rules of conduct. They had, of course, not made
it clear to themselves by thought that even for thought itself
this world is nothing. Those who could say: our citizenship is in
heaven, we have no permanent abode here but we seek the future
one; those whose first principle was to die to the world, to be born
anew, and already here to enter into a new life doubtlessly gave not
the slightest value to anything sensible. They were, to use the
expression of the schools, transcendental idealists in practice.

Others who, apart from acting in accordance with their senses, as
is innate in us all, have become further strengthened and en-
meshed in sensuousness by their thought and have, as it were,
grown together with it, can raise themselves above it permanently
and completely only by persistent and consequential thought.
Without that they would always be dragged down again by their
understanding, even though their moral sentiments were the
purest, and their whole nature would remain an ever continued
insoluble contradiction. For them that philosophy, which I only
now fully understand, will be the first power to free Psyche from
her cocoon and spread her wings, on which she first hovers above
herself and casts a last glance at the abandoned husk, thereafter to
live and move in higher spheres.

Blessed be the hour in which I decided to reflect on myself and
my vocation. All my questions are answered; I know what I can
know, and I don't worry about what I can't know. I am satisfied.
There is perfect harmony and clarity in my mind and a new and
splendid existence begins for me.

I do not comprehend my whole complete vocation; what I ought to become and what I will be transcends all my thought. A part of this vocation is hidden from me. It is visible only to one, the father of spirits, to whom it is entrusted. I only know that it is surely mine, that it is eternal and splendid like He himself. That part of it, however, which is entrusted to me I know. I know it thoroughly, and it is the root of all my other knowledge. At every moment of my life I know for certain what I ought to do at that moment: and this is my whole vocation so far as it depends on me. I must not deviate from that, since my knowledge does not extend beyond it. I ought not to want to know anything beyond it. I ought to take a firm stand on this one central point and take root there. All my effort and striving and my whole ability are to be directed toward it. My whole existence is to be involved in it.

I ought to cultivate my understanding and acquire as much knowledge as I possibly can; but with the sole intention of giving duty a greater scope in me thereby, and of giving it a wider sphere of activity. I ought to want to have much so that much can be demanded of me. I ought to exercise my strength and skill in every respect, but only so as to provide duty with a more useful and skillful tool in me. For until the commandment enters the external world from out of my whole person I am responsible to my conscience for it. I ought to display humanity to its fullest in myself as far as I am capable, but not for the sake of humanity itself. Humanity is in itself not of the slightest value. I should do it, rather, in order that virture, which alone has intrinsic value, may be displayed to its highest perfection in humanity. I ought to regard myself, body and soul and with all that is in me, only as a means to duty, and ought to be concerned only to do my duty, and that I *can* do it so far as in me lies. As soon as the commandment—if only it really is the commandment which I have obeyed, and if only I am really conscious of the one pure intention of obeying it—as soon as the commandment enters the world from out of my person, I have no longer to be concerned, for from there on it enters into the hand of the eternal will. Any further concern would be an idle self-inflicted torment, would be unbelief and mistrust of that will. It should never occur to me to want to rule the world in its stead, to listen to the voice of my limited cleverness instead of its voice in my conscience, and to put the one-sided plan of a shortsighted individual into the place of its plan which extends over the whole. I know that

I would thereby necessarily drop out of its order and from that of all spiritual beings.

As I honor this higher dispensation with calm devotion, so I ought to honor the freedom of other beings outside me in my conduct. The question is not what *they* ought to do in my opinion, but rather what *I* may do to move them to do it. But I can seek directly to influence only their conviction and their will, so far as the order of society and their own consent permit it; but I must not want to act on their strength and their circumstances without their agreement and their will. Where I cannot or may not change it, they do what they do on their own responsibility, and the eternal will will direct everything to the best. It is more important to me to respect their freedom than to hinder or prevent what seems to me evil in the use of it.

I raise myself to this standpoint and am a new creature, and my whole relationship to the present world is transformed. The ties by which my mind was so far attached to this world, and through whose secret tug it followed all movements in it, are cut forever, and I stand free and calm and unmoved, myself my own world. It is no longer with the heart that I apprehend objects and connect with them, but only with the eye; and this eye itself is clarified in freedom and sees through error and deformity to the true and the beautiful, just as shapes are reflected pure and in a milder light on an unruffled water's surface.

My mind is forever closed to perplexity and confusion, to uncertainty, to doubt and anxiety; my heart to sorrow, to regret, to desire. I care to know only one thing: what I ought to do, and this I always know infallibly. About all else I know nothing, and know that I know nothing about it, and sink firm roots into this my ignorance, and refrain from having any opinions, from making any conjectures, and from coming to be at odds with myself over something I know nothing about. No event in the world can move me through joy or through sorrow; cold and untouched I look down on them all, for I know that I can understand the meaning of none, nor see its connection with what alone matters to me. All that happens belongs in the plan of the eternal world and *is* good in it so far as I know. What is pure gain in this plan, and what is only a means for doing away with present evil, and should therefore gladden me more or less, I don't know. Everything prospers in its world. That is enough for me, and in this faith I stand firm as a rock. But what in its world is only germ, what blossom, and what the fruit itself, I don't know.

The one thing which can matter to me is the progress of reason and morality in the realm of rational beings; and that simply for its own sake, for the sake of progress. Whether *I* am the instrument in this, or *another;* whether it is my deed which succeeds or is hindered, or that of another, is quite indifferent to me. I everywhere regard myself only as one of the instruments of the purpose of reason, and respect and love myself and take an interest in myself only as such, and wish my deed to succeed only so far as it aims at this purpose. I therefore regard all world events in quite the same way only in respect of this one purpose; whether they originate in me or in others, whether they relate directly to me or to others. My breast is closed to annoyance over personal affronts and offenses and to the promotion of personal merit; for my whole personality has long gone and disappeared in the contemplation of the goal.

I will not be disconcerted if ever it should seem as though truth has now been completely silenced and that virtue is to be annihilated, as though unreason and vice have this time mustered all their strength and can simply not be prevented from counting as reason and true wisdom; if ever, just as all good men were hoping that things might go better for humanity, things should turn out worse than ever; and if ever the work, well and happily begun with the eyes of good men on it in joyful hope, should suddenly and unexpectedly turn into the utmost disgrace. And just as little will it make me lazy and careless and secure, as though everything had now succeeded, if at another time it seems that suddenly enlightenment is growing and prospering, that freedom and independence are spreading rapidly, and that milder customs, peacefulness, agreeableness, and general fairness are increasing among men. So it seems to me. Indeed it *is* so, it really is so for me; and I know in both cases, as well as in all possible cases, what else I now have to do. About everything else I remain perfectly calm, for I know nothing about everything else. Those events which seem so sad to me could, in the plan of the eternal one, be the nearest means to a very good result. That battle of evil against good may be meant to be its last significant battle, and it may be allowed this time to gather all its strength in order to lose it and to step into the light in all its impotence. Those appearances which please me so may rest on very dubious grounds. What I took to be enlightenment may perhaps be mere sophistry, cleverness, and aversion to all ideas. What I took to be independence may only be lasciviousness and lack of self-control. What I took to be mildness and peacefulness may be indolence and laxity. I don't now this, of course, but it could be so, and I would then have just as little reason to be sad about the former as to be glad about the latter. But this I know, that I am in the world of the highest wisdom and goodness which completely sees through its plan and carries it out infallibly; and I rest in this conviction and am happy.

No more can it disconcert me and consign me to the power of resentment and indignation that it is free beings, destined to reason and morality, who fight against reason and expend their energy in the promotion of unreason and vice. The perversity of having hated the good because it is good and promoted evil from the pure love of evil as such, which alone could arouse my just anger, I do not ascribe to anyone with human features; for I know that it does not lie in human nature. I know that for all who act this way, so far as they act this way, there is no good and evil at all, but only pleasant and unpleasant. Such people are not in control of themselves but are in the power of nature. It is not they, but nature in them, which seeks the pleasant with all its power and flees the unpleasant without any consideration of whether it is also good or evil. I know that, once they are what they are, they cannot in the least behave otherwise than they do; and I am far from waxing indignant against necessity or from being angry with blind nature devoid of will. Of course, it is their fault and disgrace that they are what they are and that, instead of being free and being something for themselves, they give themselves up to the stream of blind nature.

This alone could have annoyed me; but here I fall into the midst of absolute incomprehensibility. I cannot ascribe a lack of freedom to them without already presupposing that they are free to make themselves free. I want to be angry with them and find no object for my anger. What they really are does not deserve this anger; what would deserve it, they are not; and if they were, then again they would not deserve it. My annoyance would be aimed at what is evidently nothing. Of course, I must always treat them and speak with them as though they were free, knowing very well that they are not. Only on the presupposition of freedom can I confront them and have to do with them, and so I must constantly presuppose it. Duty commands one conception of them for my activity, while observation gives me the opposite conception. And so it may happen that I turn against them with noble indignation, as though they were free, in order to inflame them against themselves with this indignation, an indignation which rationally I can never feel even inwardly. It is only the acting social man in me who is angry with unreason and vice, not the observing man who is self-sufficient and complete within himself.

I will not be able to avoid *feeling* physical suffering, pain, and illness, if I should be visited by them, for they are events of my nature and here below I am and remain nature; but they shall not *dismay* me. They touch only the nature with which I am connected in some wondrous way, not me myself, the being exalted above all nature. The certain end of all pain and all susceptibility to pain is death; and among all those things which the natural man is accustomed to regard as evil, I take this to be the least. I won't die at all for *myself,* but only for *others,* for those who remain behind from whose midst I am torn. For me the hour of death is the hour of birth into a new and more splendid life.

Once my heart is closed to all desire for earthly things, once I really no longer have any attachment to transitory things, the universe appears to me transformed and purified. The dead inert mass, which was only the stuffing of space, has disappeared, and in its place there flows and surges and rushes the eternal stream of life and power and deeds—the stream of original life; of your life, Eternal One: for all Life is your life, and only the religious eye penetrates to the realm of true beauty.

I am your kin, and what I see round about me is related to me; everything is animated and besouled and looks at me through bright spirit eyes and speaks to my heart with spirit sounds. In all forms outside of me I see myself again, divided and separated in myriad ways, and I shine back at myself from them, like the morning sun which shines back at itself broken in myriad ways in a thousand dewdrops.

Your life, as a finite being may think of it, is a willing which simply forms and presents itself through itself. This life, made manifoldly sensible to mortal eye, flows down through me into all of immeasureable nature. Here it flows through my veins and muscles as self-producing, self-forming matter, and outside of me deposits its bounty in trees, plants, and grass. Formative life flows as *one* continuous stream, drop by drop, in all forms and wherever my eye can follow it. And it looks at me differently from every point of the universe, as the same force through which in secret darkness it forms my own body. There it surges freely, and leaps and dances as self-forming movement in the animal, and presents itself in each new body as another independent, self-sufficient world: the same force which, invisible to me, stirs and moves in my own limbs. Everything which moves follows this general trait, this single principle of all movement, which conducts the harmonious tremor from one end of the universe to the other: the animal without freedom; I, from whom movement originates in the visible world without thereby having its source in me, with freedom.

But pure and holy, and as close to your essential being as anything can be in the eyes of mortals, your life flows on as the bond which ties spirit to spirit in unity, as air and ether of the one world of reason; unthinkable and incomprehensible, and yet lying open to the spiritual eye. Borne along in this stream of light thought floats unhindered and remaining the same from soul to soul, and returns purer and transfigured from the kindred breast. Through this secret the individual finds himself and understands and loves himself only in another; and every spirit separates itself only from other spirits, and there is no human being but only one humanity, no individual thinking and loving and hating, but only one thinking and loving and hating in and through each other. Through this secret the kinship of spirits in the invisible world streams forth into their physical nature, and presents itself in two sexes which, even if every spiritual bond could break, are already compelled to love each other as natural beings. The kinship of spirits flows out into the tenderness of parents and children and siblings, as though souls also were born of one blood, like bodies, and minds were branches and blossoms of the same tree; and from there, in narrower and wider circles, it embraces the whole sentient world. The thirst for love is the foundation even of their hatred, and no enmity arises except from failed friendship.

Through what appears to others as dead mass my eye sees this eternal life and movement in all veins of sensible and spiritual nature; and it sees this life constantly increasing and growing and purifying itself for its own more spiritual self-expression. The universe no longer seems to me that circle returning into itself, that endlessly repeating game, that monster which devours itself so as to give birth to itself again as it already was. For my eyes it has become spiritualized and bears the mark proper to spirit: constant progress to greater perfection in a straight line which goes on to infinity.

The sun rises and sets, and the stars sink and come again, and all spheres carry on their circle-dance. But they never come back as they disappeared, and in the shining sources of life there is already life and growth. Every hour brought on by them, every morning and every evening descends upon the world with new growth; new life and new love rain down from the spheres like dewdrops from a cloud, and embrace nature like a cool night embracing the earth.

All death in nature is birth, and precisely in dying does the augmentation of life visibly appear. There is no killing principle in nature, for nature is throughout nothing but life. It is not death which kills, but rather a more living life which, hidden behind the old life, begins and develops. Death and birth are only the struggle of life with itself in order to present itself ever more purely and more like itself. And how could *my* death be anything else? For I am not a mere representation and image of life, but bear within me the original life which alone is true and essential. That nature might destroy a life which does not come from nature is not even a possible thought; nature, for whose sake I do not live, but which itself lives merely for my sake.

But it cannot destroy even my natural life, even this mere presentation to finite sight of the inner invisible life, because to do so it would have to be capable of destroying itself; nature, which only exists for me and for my sake, and does not exist if I don't. Precisely because nature kills me it must bring me to life again; it can only be my higher life, developing within nature, before which my present life disappears; and what the mortal calls death is the visible appearance of a second coming to life. If no rational being on earth, having once seen its light, were to die, there would be no reason to await a new heaven and a new earth: the only possible intention of this nature, to present and preserve reason, would already be fulfilled here below and its circumference would be closed. But the act by which it kills a free independent being is its festive passing beyond this act and beyond the whole sphere which it thereby closes with this step, a step which is evident to all reason. The appearance of death is the guide by which my spiritual eye is led to my new life and my new nature.

Each one like me who leaves the earthly association and whom my spirit cannot suppose to have been annihilated, for he is like me—each such person draws my thoughts with him beyond the present world. He still *exists,* and is entitled to a place. While we mourn him here below—as there would be mourning, if there could, in the dull realm of unconsciousness, if a human being were to escape from it into the light of the earthly sun—there is joy on the other side that a human being was born into their world, just as we citizens of earth welcome ours with joy. When one day I will follow them, there will only be joy for me; for sorrow remains behind in the sphere which I leave.

The world which but now I still admired sinks and disappears from my view. In all its fullness of life, its order and flourishing growth which I see there, it still is only the curtain which hides an infinitely more perfect world from me, and the seed from which it is to develop. My faith steps behind this curtain and warms and animates this seed. It sees nothing definite, but it expects more than it can grasp here below and will ever be able to grasp in time.

So I live and so I am, and so I am unchangeable, firm and complete for all eternity. For this is no being assumed from without. It is my own, my only true and essential being.